SIEGES

THAT CHANGED THE WORLD

ALAMO

CONSTANTINOPLE

DIEN BIEN PHU

MASADA

PETERSBURG

STALINGRAD

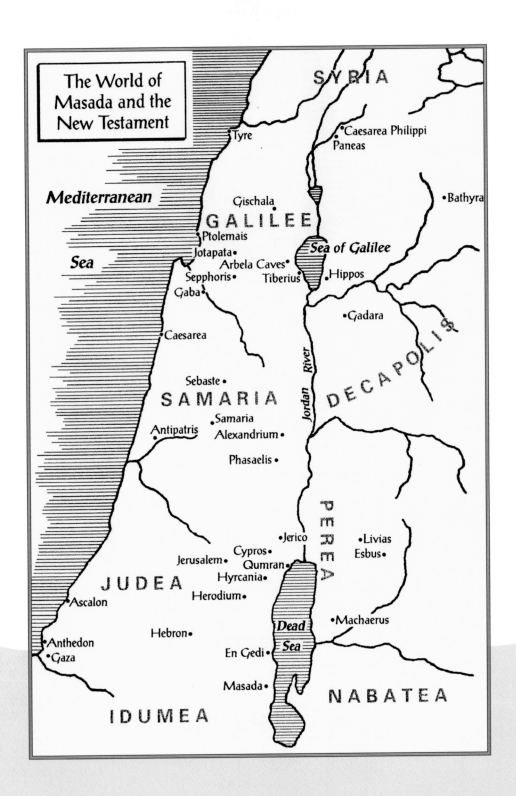

The World of Masada and the New Testament

SYRIA

Tyre

Caesarea Philippi
Paneas

Mediterranean

Bathyra

Gischala

GALILEE

Ptolemais

Sea of Galilee

Sea

Jotapata
Arbela Caves
Sepphoris   Tiberius
Gaba

Hippos

Caesarea

Gadara

DECAPOLIS

Jordan River

Sebaste

SAMARIA

Samaria
Antipatris   Alexandrium

Phasaelis

PEREA

Jerico
Cypros   Livias
Jerusalem   Qumran   Esbus
Hyrcania
Herodium

JUDEA

Ascalon

Machaerus

Hebron

Dead
Anthedon   Sea
Gaza   En Gedi

Masada   NABATEA

IDUMEA

SIEGES
THAT CHANGED
THE WORLD

MASADA

TIM McNEESE

CHELSEA HOUSE
PUBLISHERS

A Haights Cross Communications Company

Philadelphia

FRONTIS: Map of the region around Masada.

COVER: Modern-day ruins of the mountaintop fortress of Masada.

CHELSEA HOUSE PUBLISHERS

VP, NEW PRODUCT DEVELOPMENT Sally Cheney
DIRECTOR OF PRODUCTION Kim Shinners
CREATIVE MANAGER Takeshi Takahashi
MANUFACTURING MANAGER Diann Grasse

STAFF FOR MASADA

EXECUTIVE EDITOR Lee Marcott
ASSOCIATE EDITOR Bill Conn
PRODUCTION EDITOR Jaimie Winkler
PICTURE RESEARCHER Pat Burns
SERIES & COVER DESIGNER Keith Trego
LAYOUT 21st Century Publishing and Communications, Inc.

A Haights Cross Communications ⭢ Company

http://www.chelseahouse.com

First Printing

1 3 5 7 9 8 6 4 2

Library of Congress Cataloging-in-Publication Data

McNeese, Tim.
   Masada / Timothy McNeese.
      p. cm.—(Sieges that changed the world)
Includes index.
Contents: The people of Yahweh—Herod builds Masada—The Jews rise
up—The siege of Jotapata—Destruction in Jerusalem—The last strong-
hold—Masada awaits discovery.
   ISBN 07910-7103-0
   1. Jews—History—168 B.C.–135 A.D.—Juvenile literature. 2 Jews—
History—Rebellion, 66–73—Juvenile literature. 3. Masada Site (Israel)—
Siege, 72–73—Juvenile literature. 4. Masada Site (Israel)—Juvenile
literature. 5 Palestine—History—To 70 A.D.—Juvenile literature.
[1. Jews—History—168 B.C.–135 A.D. 2. Jews—History—Rebellion,
66–73. 3. Masada Site (Israel)—Siege, 72–73. 4. Palestine—History—
To 70 A.D.] I. Title. II Series.
DS122 .M465 2002
933' .05—dc21

                                          2002012918

TABLE OF CONTENTS

The People
of Yahweh

Jewish Zealots, who were resisting the oppressive rule of the Roman Empire, held out against Roman forces at the mountaintop fortress of Masada in A.D. 73.

Below the 1,300-foot (396-meter) summit, perched atop a bleak, rocky outcropping, a mass of 15,000 people—many of them Roman soldiers, the rest Jewish captives from earlier military encounters—prepared to bring about the fall of a ragtag garrison. The garrison was full of Zealots, those who believed in an independent Jewish state, who were occupying the ancient Jewish fortress town called Masada. The lengthy siege, which may have lasted a full seven months, was about to come to an end. Roman troops and engineers had erected a huge ramp up one side of the well-defended fortress. An iron-tipped battering ram had pounded the Masada walls relentlessly until part of the defensive perimeter had collapsed in a dusty heap, leaving a breach in the

Zealots' defenses and an open invitation for Roman troops to attack.

That evening, the Roman general, Flavius Silva, prepared his men to launch a massive assault the next morning in the hopes that they could bring down the last Jewish stronghold challenging Roman authority and power in the ancient Near Eastern lands of the collapsed kingdom of Judea. Other Jewish cities and fortresses—including Jerusalem itself—had fallen to Roman sieges over the previous six years of conflict. Now Masada stood alone, as it made a defiant last stand against the Romans.

On the mountaintop, tired and beleaguered Jewish Zealots considered their options now that an attack seemed inevitable. Below, in the distance, the shimmering waters of the Dead Sea glistened under the rays of a setting sun that might well be the last these rebel fighters would ever see. Perhaps they could escape under cover of darkness, some must have thought. Negotiate, others might have suggested, or all would be lost. Then, there were others who surely believed there was no choice but to die defending their positions, rather than be taken prisoner by the Romans.

The leader of the Zealots, however, a warrior known to history as Eleazar Ben Ya'ir, presented his fellow freedom fighters with yet another option, a final act of Jewish defiance in the face of certain annihilation at the hands of the Romans. Time was running out. The last defenders of Masada would have to make a choice.

The Jewish people who stood against the Romans on the summit of Masada were the inheritors of 2,000 years of recorded Hebrew history. Jews trace their ancestry through a wealthy nomadic shepherd named Abraham, who lived in the eastern end of the Fertile Crescent, a vast region of the ancient world known for its agriculture, extensive trade systems, and early cities. Today, this region is home to the

The Bible tells the story of how the ancestors of the Jewish peoples, Abraham and his descendants, moved to Canaan, where they lived as farmers and shepherds. Abraham and his family are seen on their way to Canaan in this Renaissance-era painting.

Middle Eastern countries of Iraq, Syria, Jordan, and Israel. According to the Bible, which is a holy book to both Jews and Christians today, Abraham migrated around 1900 B.C. from his home in Ur of Mesopotamia and settled in Canaan, a land already occupied by other warrior clans, city dwellers, and sea peoples living along the eastern shores of the Mediterranean Sea. When Abraham arrived in this land, which lies at the western end of the Fertile Crescent, the city of Jerusalem was already at least 1,000 years old. It was home to the Jebusites (an early name for the urban setting was Jebu Salem, which in time became known as Jerusalem). There began the true history of the Jews, a proud people keenly aware of their historical, cultural, ethnic, and religious heritage.

From their patriarchal origins—including Abraham and his son, Isaac, as well as his grandson, Jacob—the Jews, a Semitic people in the ancient world, came to be called the Hebrews. Unlike other ancient peoples, the Hebrews believed in only one god. This fact alone has formed the centerpiece of the heritage of the Hebrews and the ongoing legacy of the Jewish people today. According to the Bible, Abraham's grandson Jacob was renamed "Israel" by the Hebrew deity, Yahweh. Israel is the name of the modern Jewish state. Jacob's 12 sons provided the origins for the Twelve Tribes of Israel, who came to be known as the Israelites.

Just as their fathers Abraham, Isaac, and Jacob had done, the tribes of Israel lived in Canaan as shepherds and farmers, raising grains and other crops. Their descendants grew in number and established a place for themselves among their Canaanite neighbors.

Over the following 500 years, the Hebrew people experienced a rich and dramatic history. According to the Bible's Old Testament, one of Jacob's younger sons, Joseph, was sold into Egyptian slavery by his brothers, who believed that he was their father's favorite. Through extraordinary circumstances, Joseph rose through the social ranks and became a chief advisor to the Egyptian pharaoh (ruler). After reconciling with his brothers, Joseph moved his entire family of the Israelites to Egypt, where they grew in number over hundreds of years.

By the 1400s B.C. (some scholars place the date in the 1200s), Egyptian leaders, fearful of the growing population of those they referred to as the "Hapiru," enslaved the descendants of Joseph. From among their ranks, a leader named Moses finally emerged. According to the Hebrew Old Testament, Moses led his people out of Egypt against the will of the pharaoh. This escape from Egyptian bondage, known today as the Exodus, is the most important milestone in the history of the Jewish people. From the story of the Exodus, come the Jewish festival of Passover, the origins of Hebrew laws, the Ten Commandments, and Levitical law.

Moses, according to the Old Testament, did not live to deliver his people back into the lands of Canaan to the northeast of Egypt. His successor, a military leader named Joshua, finished the journey, but only after decades of wandering in the desert regions of the Sinai peninsula.

For 200 years, the Israelites struggled to reestablish their home in Canaan, carrying out military conquests and skillfully negotiating peace treaties and trade alliances with the Canaanite peoples. Often divided among themselves and drawn into intertribal conflicts, the Israelites finally subdued many of their neighbors in Canaan. This allowed for the creation of an Israelite kingdom that ruled over the Canaanite region.

For over 100 years, from the eleventh to the tenth century B.C., the Israelite kingdom—ruled by three Hebrew kings known as Saul, David, and Solomon—prospered and grew in the ancient world. Though it never developed into a strong, extensive empire, the Israelite kingdom was dominant regionally and held an important geographical position along the widely used trade routes that spanned the Fertile Crescent. While Jews today consider King David to be the Israelite king, his son, Solomon, built an elaborate temple to Yahweh in Jerusalem. The temple in Jerusalem became the center of Jewish religious life and the symbolic capital of the Hebrew faith. Of equal importance to the ancient Israelites was their holy book, the Torah, which was made up of the first five books of the Bible. The written word of the Torah provided direction, history, and symbolism for the developing religion of Judaism.

The reigns of the first three kings of Israel represented

a golden era in the history of the Israelites, but the power of the kingdom of Israel fell after the death of Solomon. By 922 B.C., the tribes of Israel had divided, and each was led by its own king. The ten northern tribes kept the kingdom of Israel, while two southern tribes, Benjamin and Judah, created a kingdom called Judah. The Israelite capital of Jerusalem remained the capital of this southern kingdom. (It is from the tribal name "Judah" that the word *Jew* was derived.)

The two kingdoms were ruled separately by two different kings. Still, the Hebrew people remained united in their faith, clinging to the teachings of Moses and worshiping Yahweh. Over the next two centuries, the history of the two neighboring kingdoms of Hebrew people saw the Hebrews forsake their religion and practice the beliefs of their Canaanite neighbors, which included idol worship and even child sacrifice. Even though several important prophets—including Elijah, Isaiah, and Jeremiah—warned the people of the evils of turning away from the religion of their heritage and Yahweh, the power and regional significance of the two kingdoms spiraled downward until the unthinkable occurred.

In the 700s B.C., the people of the northern kingdom of Israel were overrun by an aggressive empire to the north, Assyria. The Assyrians were a cruel, militaristic people who sometimes skinned their captives alive. Once the kingdom of Israel was conquered by the Assyrians, many Israelites were taken captive and removed from their homelands, scattered throughout the lands then under Assyrian rule. Many of these uprooted Hebrew people never returned to the lands of their ancestors. They disappeared into the pages of history as they intermarried with non-Hebrew neighbors. Today, these former Hebrew peoples are referred to as the Ten Lost Tribes of Israel.

By the 580s B.C., the southern kingdom of Judah also

fell, in this case to the Babylonians. These Mesopotamian invaders destroyed the sacred temple in Jerusalem and removed many Hebrew people from their homeland, taking them back to Babylon. Unlike the Assyrians' conquest, which managed to destroy the Jewish culture of the Ten Tribes, the Babylonian captivity lasted just a little more than a generation. The relatively short duration allowed even those who had been taken from Judah to keep their religion and culture intact. In 539 B.C., Persian King Cyrus defeated the Babylonians and inherited the dispossessed people known as the Jews. Cyrus was a kinder, gentler emperor than other royal invaders had been. He allowed the Jews to return to the land of Judah.

Once there, they immediately set about rebuilding the ruined Temple of Jerusalem. Not all Jews, however, went back to Judah. Some remained in Babylon, while still others were scattered throughout many corners of the ancient world. Between 520 and 445 B.C., the Jews who returned to Judah rebuilt their temple and the walls of the city of Jerusalem. It was a period of rediscovery for many Jews; a time to reconnect with their homeland, the place where they believed Yahweh lived. They restored their old laws and reestablished their traditional Hebrew worship. Some rulers—those who governed Jerusalem on behalf of the Persians, such as Nehemiah—were experts in Jewish law. Nehemiah enforced the Sabbath observance and tried to keep the Jews from marrying foreigners.

By the fourth century B.C., Persia fell under the dominance of another power of the ancient world. A ruler of the kingdom of Macedon (located on the Balkan Peninsula), Alexander the Great, marched his well-trained armies to the East, and captured Judea and Jerusalem in 332 B.C. Alexander was one of the greatest of the ancient generals. He conquered the Persian Empire, including the lands of Egypt, Mesopotamia, Anatolia, Phoenicia, and Palestine, which included Judah, or Judea. As Alexander established the biggest Near East empire in history prior to the Romans, he spread the influence of the Greek, or Hellenistic, world from which he came across the lands he defeated. Within a few years, Alexander ruled a huge, sprawling Hellenistic Empire whose subjects learned Greek philosophy, religion, culture, art, architecture, and politics. Greek, which became the common language of the Hellenistic world, even made a direct impact on the Jewish religion when the first Greek translation of the Old Testament, a version known as the Septuagint, was produced.

More serious changes were also forced on the Jews living in Judah, however. After the death of Alexander, who died in 323 B.C., possibly of malaria, his Hellenistic Empire was divided between the Macedonian emperor's generals. The eastern portion became the center of a rivalry between the Egyptian ruler Ptolemy and the ruler of Alexander's Asian lands, Seleucus. Both men claimed dominion over Judah, the lands known to the Greeks as Palestine. After Ptolemy I captured Jerusalem in 320 B.C., Egypt controlled Palestine for about a century. Following in the path of the Persians, the Ptolemies (Ptolemy I and his descendants) did not force significant changes on religion or culture in Palestine. The Jews lived in peace and remained true to their own heritage. They prospered, too. The Ptolemies allowed the Jewish high priest of the Temple in Jerusalem to serve as the religious head of Palestine, as well as the governmental leader of the Jewish state.

Then, in 198 B.C., the Seleucids (the rulers of Seleucus's camp) gained control of Palestine after they defeated the Ptolemies. The Seleucid ruler, Antiochus III, also known as Antiochus the Great (223–187 B.C.), supported the Jews. He dealt kindly with them and provided financial support to help rebuild their cultural and religious center, Jerusalem. Antiochus III even exempted the Jews from taxation for three years after he gained control of Palestinian territory. Yet, while the Jews remained free to pursue their traditional religion and cultural activities, a radical change was taking place among Jews who enjoyed wealth, power, and influence.

Through 150 years of continual exposure to Greek culture, some Jews became hellenized. This meant they accepted the "Greekification" of their culture, and even their religion. They took on the ways of the Greeks despite the disapproval of many of their fellow Jews, who wanted to remain true to their heritage of faith and practice. Since many of these so-called hellenizers held positions of authority and power, their decisions sometimes set the course for others. One such hellenizer was a high priest named Jason. He bought his office, the most important position in Palestine, and began to transform Jerusalem into a Greek city-state. With the support of wealthy patrons, Jason ordered the construction of a gymnasium—a type of complex known for activities that traditional Jews would have found unacceptable. Historian Menahem Stern, writing in *A History of the Jewish People*, explained the significance of the Greek institution on the Jews:

> The atmosphere surrounding the gymnasium gave serious offence to Jews who had kept to their faith, for the traditions of the gymnasium were rooted in Greek paganism. . . . While it is unlikely that Jason actually introduced the cult of foreign gods in Jerusalem, the atmosphere that the gymnasium imposed on Jerusalem must have been imbued with paganism. It did not take long for the gymnasium to replace the Temple as the focus of Jerusalem's social life.

The gymnasium provided an arena for competitive games that were popular among the ancient Greeks. They were such a draw for many Jews that even priests attended the gymnasium games, leaving their Temple duties undone.

When a new Seleucid ruler, Antiochus IV, rose to the throne in 175 B.C., the Jews in Jerusalem faced a new and greater challenge. Significant changes had occurred in the Seleucid Empire even before Antiochus IV came to power. The Romans, an expansive Mediterranean people from the West, were on the march, working to conquer the entire Mediterranean region. They defeated the Seleucid kingdom of Antiochus III in 189 B.C. Following the death of Antiochus two years later, the Seleucid Empire stood on shaky ground. After the assassination of Antiochus III's son, Seleucus IV, his uncle seized power, even though Seleucus had had a son who was the legitimate heir. This new Seleucid ruler—Antiochus IV, who ruled from 175 to 164 B.C.—soon forced radical changes on the Jews within his dominion.

Antiochus IV was determined to complete the process of hellenization among the Jews. To that end, he tried to outlaw the Jewish religion by banning "the offering of the traditional sacrifices, the observance of the Sabbath, and . . . he had the holy books destroyed." He desecrated the Temple of Jerusalem by ordering the erection of an altar to the Greek god, Zeus. These acts deeply outraged many Jews. Then, to make matters worse, the Seleucid ruler garrisoned troops in Jerusalem in a citadel he had constructed called the Akra. His troops could now be seen on the streets of the Jewish city. When, in 167, Antiochus ordered all Jews to offer pagan sacrifices to Greek gods, however, the Jews had had enough. A rebellion broke out, which ultimately brought an end to Seleucid rule in Palestine.

The leader of the rebellion was a devout Jewish priest named Mattathias who lived in the Palestinian town of Modein. He was the head of a household known as the Hasmonaeans. When a Seleucid official ordered the people of Modein to perform pagan sacrifices, Mattathias refused. He was so determined to defy Seleucid power that he not only killed the Seleucid official, but also a fellow Jew who had agreed to perform the sacrifices. Once stories of Mattathias and his five sons' open defiance of the authority of Antiochus IV spread across Palestine, other bands of resistance rose up, prepared to bring down the Seleucids or die trying. Soon, followers of Mattathias were carrying out raids and murders against the Seleucids. They killed Jews as well, if they cooperated with authorities.

When Mattathias died in 166 B.C., one of his five sons, Judas, took over the leadership of the Jewish revolt. Judas, who became known as Maccabeus, which meant "the hammer," directed guerrilla warfare against both the Syrian forces of Antiochus IV and the Jews who helped this foreign power. By 164 B.C., the Maccabean revolutionaries had liberated the city of Jerusalem from Antiochus IV's rule.

In the wake of the rebels' victory, the Temple was purified and rededicated to the Jewish god, Yahweh. The festival of the dedication is still celebrated by Jews today as Hanukkah. For the first time in hundreds of years of Jewish history, bands of rebels bound by their Hebrew faith had fought for and won their freedom from a controlling power. Such groups of militarized Jews, called Zealots, would form frequently in later Jewish history.

For the next century, the Jews ruled themselves as an independent state. After the death of Judas in 160 B.C., one of Judas's brothers, Jonathan (160–143), took command of Jewish forces. Another brother, Simon (143–134) succeeded him and became not only the military commander, but the high priest in the Temple of Jerusalem. During his rule, the last of the Syrians were removed from their fortress at Akra

After the death of his father, Mattathias, Judas Maccabeus, seen here in a fifteenth-century Italian painting, took over leadership of the Jewish rebellion.

and the garrison facility was destroyed. In 134, Simon was murdered. Three Maccabean brothers ruled after him, and then Palestine continued under the direction of the Hasmonaean Dynasty, which lasted from 134 to 63 B.C.

The Origins of a Jewish Celebration

Today, modern Jews have a special tradition called the Festival of Lights, or Hanukkah. For eight days, beginning sometime between the end of November and the last days of December, Jews recall an event that took place during the Maccabean revolt in the 160s B.C. The story is a fascinating one that, according to devout Jews, centers around a miracle.

Following their defeat over the Syrians, the Maccabees reentered the Jewish Temple in Jerusalem only to find that it had been defiled by their enemies. The Syrians had entered rooms that only Jewish priests were permitted to enter and had placed Greek symbols and statues inside the holy building. Antiochus had put these objects—including a statue of himself—inside the Temple, and had ordered the Jews to bow down to them. Before the sacred grounds could be used again as a site of Jewish worship and sacrifice, they would have to be cleansed and rededicated.

The Jews set to work cleaning and repairing the Temple. When their work was completed, they prepared to rededicate the holy site. When they did so, the Maccabees celebrated the first Jewish Hanukkah. The word Hanukkah is a Hebrew word for "dedication." The day set for the rededication was the twenty-fifth day of Kislev on the Hebrew calendar.

During the rededication ceremony, the Jews intended to rekindle the menorah, a special candelabra that symbolized the relationship between God and the Jewish people. However, the Jews could find only enough undefiled oil to light the menorah for one night. The problem was that, once lit, the Temple menorah, known as the N'er Tamid, or "eternal light," was not supposed to be allowed to burn out, and it would take eight more days to produce more oil.

Then, the miracle of Jewish tradition occurred. The menorah was lit and, despite the small amount, the precious oil continued to burn for another eight days!

Today, Jewish people celebrate Hanukkah to recognize their victory over the Syrians and the rededication of the Temple in Jerusalem. In the United States, Hanukkah traditions include lighting a special menorah, giving gifts, eating designated foods, and enjoying the company of family and friends.

This era of Jewish history witnessed the administrations of five rulers, beginning with the son of Simon Maccabeus, John Hyrcanus I (134–104 B.C.).

Through the years of Maccabean leadership, the Judean state grew and prospered, finding security through treaties the Maccabean brothers made with the increasingly powerful Roman Republic. These Maccabean military-governors were able to conquer neighboring lands, capturing and subduing north Samaria and Galilee. To the south, the Jews took control of Idumaea, as well as Peraea, located east of the long, winding Jordan River. In the mountains of eastern Idumaea stood the summit of Masada. Under John Hyrcanus I, the Jews forced the Idumaeans and the Peraeans to swear allegiance to them and to adopt the Jewish religion. The rule of Hyrcanus was exemplary, and was often compared to the reign of King David nearly 1,000 years earlier.

Hyrcanus's son, Aristobulus, followed his father as ruler of Palestine and adopted the title of king. Those who followed him to the throne did the same. Aristobulus was a brutal usurper. He seized the throne from his mother, whom Hyrcanus had named as his heir. Aristobulus imprisoned his mother and left her to starve to death. He also jailed three of his brothers. A fourth brother was killed under his orders.

Aristobulus died after ruling for just one year. His wife, Salome, immediately released her husband's siblings from prison and appointed one of them, Alexander Jannaeus (103–76 B.C.) to the throne. She and Alexander were then married. Alexander reigned for nearly 30 years. A harsh ruler, he extended his kingdom's territory until he was defeated by the Nabataeans, who lived southeast of the Dead Sea. His failure led to a rebellion in his homeland by a sect of Jews called the Pharisees. Alexander put down the revolt with a vengeance. At one point, he ordered 800

Pharisees crucified in view of his palace in Jerusalem, as he and the women of his harem watched for their own amusement. Few of Palestine's people mourned when Alexander Jannaeus died after a generation of bloody rule.

After her husband's death, Salome took the throne and appointed her son, Hyrcanus II, as the high priest of the Temple in Jerusalem. Salome (76–69 B.C.) brought tranquillity to her kingdom. She favored the Pharisees and proved herself to be a moderate and intelligent woman. When she died at the age of 73, the kingdom witnessed a rivalry between her two sons, Hyrcanus II and Aristobulus II, over the throne. Although Hyrcanus was the eldest, Aristobulus defeated him.

Aristobulus (69–63) took the throne and the title of high priest, but within two years, he faced an enormous challenge—an invasion from Rome. Soon, the history of the Jewish people of Palestine would go through extraordinary change. An era of Roman dominance—something the Jews would never fully accept—was about to begin.

Herod the Great, king of the Jews, oversaw the construction of several impressive projects, including an elaborate temple built around 20 B.C. This is a scale model of Herod's Temple of Jerusalem.

Herod Builds Masada

By the first century B.C., Roman generals were advancing throughout the Mediterranean region, conquering every nation in their path. In 67 B.C., the famous Roman general, Pompey, was marching throughout the eastern regions. As Pompey reached Syria to the north, both Aristobulus and his deposed brother Hyrcanus realized what was coming. Each attempted to ally with the imperialistic Romans. As his ally, Pompey chose Hyrcanus—whom the Roman general determined would be the easier of the two brothers to control. Aristobulus did not surrender peacefully, though. His troops occupied the city of Jerusalem and Aristobulus took refuge in the Temple. Pompey continued toward Jerusalem, then besieged the holy grounds for three months in 63 B.C. A century after the days of Judas Maccabeus, the Hasmonaean Dynasty fell. Jerusalem was in the hands of the Romans

After the capture of Aristobulus and the fall of the Jerusalem Temple, Pompey acted on his curiosity. He knew that the regulations of the Temple did not allow anyone entrance except Jewish priests. Wanting to see the inside of the Temple himself, Pompey visited the holy structure and even went into the most sacred room of the Temple complex, called the Holy of Holies. Jewish belief said that this was the throne room of Yahweh. For the Romans to enter was an absolute abomination to the Jews. Pompey was guilty of sacrilege, and the Jews never forgave him for his pagan breach.

While the Romans became dominant over Palestine and the ancient city of Jerusalem, they relied on regional alliances and local rule to provide stability for Roman authority. Pompey placed Hyrcanus II on the Jewish throne, but his power and lands were greatly diminished. The Romans took the coastal lands and Samaria away from Jewish control. Syria, in fact, became a province of Rome, and its governor was granted power over Palestine. Hyrcanus was forced to answer to the governor of Syria, Gabinius.

Once the Romans came to dominate Palestine, zealous Jews attempted to rise against their conquerors. In 57 B.C., one such revolt forced Hyrcanus to appeal to Gabinius for help. After the rebellion had been smashed, Gabinius would no longer allow Hyrcanus to rule in his own right. He even took away Hyrcanus's title of king. The Syrian governor then divided Palestine into five separately governed districts. Even as Hyrcanus tried to continue to rule, power over Palestine was handed over to his chief minister, Antipater II.

Antipater was an astute politician. He sought the favor of the Romans and was rewarded for his loyalty. Yet, as one general after another began to wield power in Rome, his allegiance shifted. By 55 B.C., three Roman generals formed a three-way partnership to rule Rome. The triumvirs, as the partners were called, were Pompey; Crassus, the soon-to-be governor of Syria who saw himself as another Alexander the Great; and Julius Caesar, who marched his armies into ancient Europe to conquer the Celtic peoples. The three-way division of power did not last long, however. Crassus was killed during a military campaign. (In part, he paid for his military actions by robbing the Temple treasury in Jerusalem, an act that won him the hatred of many of the Jews.) Caesar and Pompey then fought one another, until Pompey was assassinated while in Egypt. Antipater was fortunate to have supported Caesar. He was rewarded in 47 B.C. with an appointment as procurator (an officer of the Roman Empire) of Judea. A man of true power in Roman-dominated Palestine, Antipater made his two eldest sons rulers. His son, Phasael, became governor of Jerusalem, and 25-year-old Herod was made ruler of Galilee.

When his father was poisoned and killed in 40 B.C. by political rivals, Herod captured the leader of the conspiracy and ordered his execution. During the next year, Herod faced several challenges. Julius Caesar, who had become Rome's imperial ruler, had been murdered in 44 B.C., throwing the empire into chaos and civil war as potential successors struggled for power. As political and military battle lines were drawn between various Roman strongmen, Herod attempted to choose a position for himself.

Although Herod was technically a Jew, he was highly Hellenized. He worked constantly to spread the influence

Herod the Great Builder

The better part of the legacy of Herod the Great is found in his many building projects which usually featured strong Hellenistic elements. Herod's general construction program included a completely redone Temple in Jerusalem and the establishment of a new city, the port of Caesarea (in Palestine, south of Haifa). The creation of this important town began in 22 B.C. and was not completed for another 12 years. The city included a semicircular harbor that measured nearly one-third of a mile (half a kilometer) in length with a width almost as big as three football fields. There were public baths and a sewage system. The city also boasted a theater, amphitheater-stadium, and a temple designed to pay tribute to the power of the Roman ruler, Augustus Caesar. Late in his reign, Herod the Great moved his center of government to Caesarea. The ruins of a great aqueduct remain today, from a system that delivered water to the city from the northeastern hills.

As for the Temple renovations, Herod spent many years rebuilding and restoring the Holy Temple in Jerusalem. New foundation walls were erected. He doubled the area of the Temple itself and created extensive courtyards complete with elaborate columns. As he ordered its construction, he was careful to support Jewish law, not wishing to alienate the devout Jews. With great concern for the requirements of Jewish tradition and reverence, Herod ordered 1,000 priests to be trained as stonemasons, so they could work on the Temple, since no one was allowed inside the house of God except priests. When the Temple was completed, Herod ordered 300 oxen to be sacrificed to the Hebrew god, Yahweh.

Despite his clear respect for the faith of the Jews, Herod placed a statue of a golden eagle above the Temple's main gate. This highly offended many devout Jews, because their law forbids any statuary, or "graven images." Although the new Temple was dedicated in 10 B.C., the Temple and its adjacent courts were not fully completed until A.D. 63.

While the Temple was renovated, Herod also ordered the rebuilding of the Roman fortress located north and directly adjacent to the Temple grounds. The garrison post was elaborately adorned. Herod named the new military facility "Antonia" to honor his Roman friend Mark Antony.

of Greek culture. Herod retained his power during a volatile period in the history of the region because of his undying commitment to expanding the dominance of the Roman Empire. He took part in politics with little regard to any moral limits. When it served his purposes, Herod divorced his wife, Doris, and expelled her and their son from Jerusalem. The Jews despised him for his harshness.

Herod was wise enough to know that the firm cruelty of his rule alienated many of his Jewish subjects. So he determined to construct a secure fortress to protect himself and his family, since Judean Palestine had been racked by violent rebellion on more than one occasion in Jewish history. Rather than build such a bastion in Jerusalem or some other urban center, Herod picked an obscure mountaintop bordering the western reaches of the Dead Sea.

This fortress would be able to protect Herod's family from any number of enemies. Herod knew he might one day lose the support of the Roman Empire, given the fact that generals and rulers rose and fell quite often. He had enemies elsewhere, too—leaders with a good deal of regional power, such as the ruler of Egypt, Cleopatra. To create an emergency route of escape and a place of refuge, one that could be defended perhaps indefinitely, became Herod's goal. He chose for this fortress's location a mountaintop in the desert, a site that would be known as *Masada,* which meant "fort" in Hebrew.

Herod first visited the mountain site in 42 B.C., when Hyrcanus II and Aristobulus II were struggling for control of the Hasmonean throne. A fortress had already been built there, either by Jonathan, the brother of Judas Maccabeus, or by Alexander Jannaeus, who was also known as Jonathan. Herod was sent from Jerusalem to seize Masada from a group of Jewish rebels. Two years passed before he returned to Masada, this time under completely different circumstances. This time, political rivals, with the help of an eastern people known as Parthians who were bitter enemies of Rome, attempted a coup against the Jerusalem government, Herod took his immediate family to Masada to avoid being captured and put to death. He did not stay at the mountain fortress. Instead, he left his family behind and went on to Alexandria, Egypt, and Rhodes, then to Rome to gain support to help him remove the Parthians from Judea.

In Rome, Herod got the support he wanted. He was declared king of the Jews with the approval of the Roman Senate. Several years passed, however, before he had completely secured his lands and titles. During these years, Antigonus, who was trying to take Herod's throne, laid siege to Masada, intending to capture Herod's relatives. Herod arrived in time to prevent this and drove Antigonus's army away.

Although the Herodian family had survived the ordeal at Masada, the siege had revealed some of the fundamental problems that anyone attempting to hold out on the mountain for a long period of time would have to face. For one, the people who took refuge there had nearly surrendered due to a lack of water. Fortunately, a strong storm had helped refill the fortress's water cisterns (reservoirs) just in time. Herod saw problems with the fortress walls as well and he determined to redesign the Masada hilltop into a defendable bastion that could withstand an attack by any foe. In addition, he intended to build elaborate palaces and bathing facilities.

The specific changes and improvements Herod ordered for Masada were described in the writings of a first-century Jewish historian named Josephus. Born in A.D. 37, the son of a noble Jewish family, Josephus was originally named Joseph ben Mattathias. He became a learned man, and studied Greek and Latin. He wrote an extensive history of his time. In his work, Josephus explained why Herod believed Masada was so important during his reign:

> For the report goes how Herod thus prepared this fortress on his own account, as a refuge against two kinds of dangers; the one for fear of the multitude of the Jews, lest they should depose him and restore their former kings for the government; the other danger was greater and more terrible, which arose from Cleopatra, queen of Egypt, who did not conceal her intentions, but spoke often to Antony [a Roman leader] and desired him to cut off Herod, and entreated him to bestow the kingdom of Judea upon her.

The fortress at Masada was built on a high plateau that rose 1,300 feet (396 meters) above the desert floor near the Dead Sea. The advantage of placing a fortress on top of this summit was that the mountaintop would be nearly unapproachable. The mountain had, in prehistoric times, been part of a group of hills that ringed the western edge of the Dead Sea. Eons of time had eroded the rock peak on all sides, causing it to stand alone from the other hills.

Even today, the walls of the mountain are slanted at a severe angle. This makes climbing the rock outcropping almost impossible. In some places, the cliffsides are close to being completely vertical. The mountaintop could only be reached by two routes. One was a path on the west side that was short but treacherous. The other, known as the Snake Path, meandered up the mountain's eastern slope. It, too, was narrow, difficult to climb, and extremely dangerous.

Herod's fortress at Masada, seen here, was built atop a steep mountain that rose some 1,300 feet (396 meters) high. The rugged location gave the formidable complex an added measure of security.

This 3.5-mile (5.6-kilometer) tortuous path allowed only a brave few to ascend to the peak in single file. During a siege, anyone who scaled the Snake Path would be a target for defenders above.

The historian Josephus described the immensity of the

rock outcropping known as Masada and the difficulties of approaching the mountain:

> There was a rock not small in circumference, and very high. It was surrounded with valleys of such vast depth downward, that the eye would not reach their bottoms; they were abrupt and such as no animal could walk upon, excepting at two places of the rock. . . . One of these ways [to scale the height of the rock] is called the serpent . . . and he that would walk along it must first go on one leg then on the other; there is nothing but destruction in case your feet slip.

To further fortify Masada, Herod had the perimeter walls reconstructed. The new walls were higher and actually thick enough for rooms to be built inside them. These walls were augmented by defense towers, most of which were built where the hilltop's defenses were the weakest, along the eastern and western sides.

Herod also spent enormous sums of money turning the fortress into a magnificent palace complex, which came to be called Herod's "Hanging Palace." It is a marvel of engineering that has three levels, a terrace of royal structures carved into the northern end of the Masada mountain. The uppermost palace facility was constructed on the summit itself. The other two were built as stairs down the side of the rocky cliffs. The building on the lowest level was erected about 100 feet (30.5 meters) from the top of Masada. These two lower levels could only be reached by a series of squared-off "spiral" stairs. Today, these buildings are in various states of disrepair. Only the lowest of the three is intact enough to allow archaeologists to accurately reconstruct its layout, design, and purpose. This lower level was made up of a courtyard surrounded by columns with a small attached bathroom facility.

Despite its unique design, the Hanging Palace was not Herod's only royal house at Masada. On the summit itself, he had erected a much larger building complex near the center of the western side of the mountaintop. Three smaller buildings, considered palaces by modern archaeologists, were also built. These might have housed members of Herod's family, many of whom despised one another so much that separate living spaces would have been a necessity.

The Western Palace complex was the largest of the palaces at Masada. It was a beehive of interconnected rooms, including storerooms, kitchens, workshops, and an administrative area. Although it lies in near-ruins today, some of the royal complex's mosaic floors have been unearthed by archaeologists.

One of the larger rooms in the Western Palace was Herod's private bath. Enough of the decorations and mosaic floors have survived to give the modern viewer a fairly clear idea of the strong Hellenistic influence that could be seen in Herod's palace. The king's bathroom includes a changing room. A door to the left leads into a small warming room. From there, a door leads to a hot room, where a bath was set into an alcove at the opposite end. Due to the advanced plumbing Herod included at Masada, the room and its bath water were heated by a furnace. Warm air was delivered to the appropriate rooms through clay pipes built into the plastered walls.

Other bath facilities were also constructed by Herod's engineers and architects at Masada. A large "public" bathhouse was located on the north end of the rock plateau, near the three terraces of the Hanging Palace. The building's design was similar to that of other bathhouses of this era, including the ones at Herod's palaces in Jericho and Herodium, north of Masada. The facility featured cold, warm, and hot baths, and was probably

The ruins of Herod's bathroom, which had several adjoining alcoves to provide heated air and water, can be seen in this photograph.

used by foreign dignitaries and others who visited Herod's mountaintop retreat.

During the siege of Antigonus, Herod's family had nearly exhausted their water supply. To avoid this problem in the future, when Herod designed his royal facilities at Masada, he made changes in the water delivery system. He ordered stonecutters to hack out two great cisterns, or water reservoirs, in the hard rock of a ravine that runs along Masada's northwest side. These man-made water tanks were large enough to contain 40,000 cubic yards (30,582 cubic meters) of water. Herod's engineers then placed a dam along the ravine and the Masada valley that follows the mountain's curve along the southwest end of the plateau. Then, just as the Herodians had designed aqueducts to bring water to their cities, the engineers built water systems to deliver rainwater from the ravine to Masada's cisterns. During the rainy season along the western shores of the Dead Sea, great surges of rainwater poured into the cisterns. The dam along the ravine fed one row of hand-hewn cisterns while the water runoff from the Masada valley filled the upper row of cisterns.

The entire system provided plenty of water for the various bathhouses on the Masada plateau and could support a significant population indefinitely, as long as nature provided adequate rainfall.

By 37 B.C., Herod the Great had conquered the kingdom of Judea and ruled for 33 years until 4 B.C. His domain was immense, since his military campaigns had brought together the states of Judea, Idumea, Perea, Galilee, and Jaffa. The cost of gaining his kingdom had been expensive, especially in regard to relations among his family. His court was riddled with intrigue and conspiracy, which forced Herod to take drastic action against some family members. Among the alleged conspirators against him was one of his sons, Antipater. When Herod became convinced that one of his wives, Mariamme, the grand-daughter of a high priest, had also plotted against him, he ordered her execution in 29 B.C. Two of his sons by Mariamme were also condemned and strangled.

The reign of Herod the Great brought new recognition for the Judean kingdom and a level of urban splendor that the Jewish state had not seen since the days of King Solomon. However, Herod's reign had continued only because the king enjoyed the good graces of the Roman Empire. Slowly but surely, Rome was taking hold of Judea. This hold would ultimately lead to an extremely violent outbreak of Jewish revolts within two generations of the death of Herod the Great. The great fortress he had constructed on the windswept mountaintop of Masada would play an important role in that bloody rebellion.

The era of the Jewish revolt was marked by another major event in the history of the world—the life and death of Jesus Christ and the beginnings of Christianity. It was a Roman officer in control of Jewish lands, Pontius Pilate, who arrested and condemned Christ, who is seen in this painting being brought before Pilate. The painting was done by the master of Cappenberg in the sixteenth century.

The Jews Rise Up

The reign of Herod the Great over the kingdom of the Jews lasted for 33 years. When this strong leader died in 4 B.C., Herod's Roman ally, Emperor Augustus Caesar, insisted that the kingdom be divided among Herod's three sons. The city of Jerusalem became a Roman imperial province ruled by Roman procurators who lived in Caesarea. One of these procurators, Pontius Pilate, became famous because of his appearance in the Bible's New Testament. Pilate ruled from A.D. 26–36. The ministry of Jesus Christ took place during Pilate's rule.

By A.D. 41, Herod Agrippa I, grandson of Herod the Great, was given the title of king by Roman Emperor Caligula. Eventually, Herod Agrippa ruled a kingdom that was nearly identical in size to the one his grandfather had ruled. Herod Agrippa suppressed the new religion of Christianity and, according to the account in Acts 12 of the New Testament, he even managed to imprison one of the apostles of Jesus Christ, Simon Peter, and to execute another, James.

Herod Agrippa remained allied with Rome, although this sometimes proved to be a difficult balancing act. Many of the Roman emperors were unstable men who changed their minds frequently. Many were assassinated. He determined early in his reign to rule as a Jew over the Jews. He followed Mosaic law—the law of the Jews—and supported one of the more popular religious sects, the Pharisees. "He went out of his way to look after Jewish interests even outside his own territory." Unfortunately for the Jews, Herod Agrippa died after just three years on the throne. Unlike the Jews, the Christian community did not mourn his loss.

Because his son, Herod Agrippa II, was only 16 years old when the elder Herod Agrippa died, Roman Emperor Claudius refused to give him the Jewish throne. For a time, Palestine was ruled directly by the Romans. A new Roman ruler, Cuspius Fadus, was installed in A.D. 44. With the reinstatement of direct Roman rule over Jewish Palestine, a group of Jewish Zealots began to challenge Roman authority. An uprising took place, which brought a harsh response from the second Roman procurator, Tiberius Alexander. Alexander was a Jew from Alexandria, Egypt, but he did not practice Judaism. When the Zealot revolt occurred, he ordered the capture of the two Zealot leaders, James and Simon, and had the two men crucified.

Still, Jewish antagonism toward the Roman rulers continued. In A.D. 48, when another procurator, Cumanus, was in control of Judea, an incident caused another spontaneous revolt. It took place during the Jewish holy days called Passover. Many Jews and Jewish converts had filled the city of Jerusalem for the religious festival, crowding the grounds near the Jerusalem Temple. Roman troops were stationed on-site, patrolling the crowd to keep order. One of the soldiers raised up his tunic, revealed his naked backside, and passed wind to make a joke. The offended Jewish crowd exploded. They rioted and stoned the Roman soldiers.

When Cumanus received word of the violent outburst, he was determined to put it down quickly. He sent more soldiers to the Temple grounds, which caused a general panic among the Jewish worshippers gathered there. As the heavy crowd tried to escape from the soldiers, some fell and were trampled by the terrified mob. Thousands were crushed under the feet of their fellow Jews.

Outraged protests followed, keeping tensions high in Jerusalem. When a callous Roman soldier lost his temper during a violent confrontation with Jews, he seized and set fire to a sacred scroll, further infuriating the city's Jews. The procurator intervened, ordering the arrest and execution of the offending Roman soldier. Even that did not end the anti-Roman violence. When a handful of Galileans were killed in Samaria, a neighboring land inhabited by people the Jews considered inferior, a group of angry Jews, led by two Zealots, invaded Samaria on a mission of revenge. When Cumanus heard of this advancing group, he attacked them with his cavalry, killing and capturing many of them.

Soon, Roman authorities intervened in Judea. The governor of Syria, Quadratus, ordered an investigation of the violent state of affairs and determined that the Jews were responsible for the problem. He ordered the crucifixion of all Jewish captives. When Agrippa appealed to the new Roman emperor, Claudius, the prisoners were released. Cumanus was banished for his harsh handling of the Jewish uprising, and Agrippa II, then 22 years old, received

Cumanus's kingdom as a reward. Although these events ended positively for the Jewish Zealots, the rebellious Jews had proven once again that they were a people the Roman Empire would have to watch closely.

Three years later, Emperor Claudius put Agrippa II in charge of a second, larger kingdom to the north of the Sea of Galilee, and replaced him with a former slave to the emperor, Antonius Felix. When Claudius died the following year, he was succeeded by Emperor Nero, a brash, immoral youth who cared little for the Jews. Nero retained Felix at his post as Judean procurator, despite the former slave's disastrous rule. The Jews came to hate Felix, and thousands became Jewish Zealots. Then, Felix turned on the leader of the Zealots, arresting him and shipping him off to Rome. A harsh military campaign followed, resulting in the deaths of thousands of Zealots, many of whom were crucified. Soon, the Jews were enflamed with anti-Roman passions, which brought about a further increase in the number of rebels scattered throughout the Jewish state and beyond.

Felix's heavy-handed tactics against the Jews led the Zealots to go underground to avoid persecution. Another sect, a fanatical group of Jewish assassins known as the Sicarii, challenged Roman authority by targeting Romans and pro-Roman Jewish sympathizers. The Sicarii took their name from their weapons of choice—stubby, curved knives called "sicae," which they hid easily under their robes. They stalked their victims in crowded public places, stabbing anyone they believed was a supporter of Roman power over Judea. They even killed one of the high priests of the Temple.

Those Jews who allied themselves with rebel groups such as the Zealots or the Sicarii saw the Romans as an evil authority, aided by corrupt Jewish leaders. Even the chief priests of the Jews were known for their abuse of power.

They regularly stole from the Temple treasury a tithe (small tax) that was paid by worshippers to support regular Jewish priests. Such priests were unprovided for and some were even starving to death. The combination of unacceptable conditions—Roman oppression and Jewish corruption—helped fill the ranks of rebel groups.

By the A.D. 60s, great anxiety descended on the Jews of Jerusalem and other important urban Jewish centers, such as Caesaria. The procurator Felix was replaced by one named Festus, who died after only two years in power. During those years, the economy of Judea, which had been declining for several decades, continued to worsen. The Sicarii continued to silently assassinate their enemies, Romans and Jews alike. Rulers over Jerusalem came and went rapidly. Political unrest plagued the decade. Jewish prophets, some of whom claimed to be the Jewish messiah, or savior, warned the people that disaster was coming for the city of Jerusalem. In the fall of A.D. 62, one such prophet, who was named Jesus (he was not related to Jesus of Nazareth, the founder of the Christian religion, who had been executed during the late A.D. 20s) entered Jerusalem, predicting the destruction of the city. Even after he was arrested, threatened, and beaten, he continued to announce that dire events lay ahead for the ancient Jewish city.

As law and order declined even further in Judea, Emperor Nero sent a hard-hearted enforcer named Gessius Florus, nicknamed "the hanger and flogger," to be the next procurator. Florus was a corrupt man who "plundered the land quite openly and without restraint." His actions against the Jews in Judea only fanned the flames of hatred and encouraged rebels to carry out more underground violence against both Roman and Jewish authorities. Jewish historian Josephus described Florus, stating that he "boasted openly of his own outrages against the nation. He was unbelievably cruel, with utter contempt for truth. He did not bother to cheat single individuals. He stripped whole cities, ruined whole populations, virtually granting a free hand to any villainy just as long as he was cut in for a share of the plunder." Regularly, Florus openly raided the Jerusalem Temple and stole the tithes for himself. In the spring of A.D. 66, some Jerusalem youths mocked Florus by passing a hat in the streets and asking people to donate copper coins for the greedy ruler. In response, the procurator ordered his army into the city and demanded the arrest of anyone who had insulted him. When no one came forward, Florus unleashed his troops on the city. What happened next was described by historian Peter Connolly:

> The following day a demonstration was held outside the city, opposite the palace. Two cohorts of Roman troops were coming up the road from Caesarea. They had been warned to be ready for trouble. They drew their clubs and began beating back the demonstrators. The crowds were enormous and the troops must have realized that if they were attacked in the open they would be over-whelmed. They tried to force their way through the gate and across the city to the Antonia, [a Roman garrison post situated next to the Temple]. In the narrow streets the soldiers were jostled by the angry crowd. Florus unwisely ordered out the troops in the palace to try to clear the street. This was the final straw. Violence erupted. Stones began to fly. Youths now climbed up on to the roofs and began pelting the soldiers with stones. The soldiers could make no headway and retreated to the palace.

These were tense moments for the Roman troops and for Florus. When it appeared that the street fighting might grow into a full-scale rebellion, Florus offered to remove all the Roman troops from the city except one cohort. This defused the violence for a time. Agrippa was called to Jerusalem to calm the fears of the rebellious Jews. Though the people welcomed their young king at first, they soon turned on him, once they saw that he was only interested in reducing the level of violence. When he did not give the Jews his full support, they ordered him out of the city.

For some Jews, these events signaled a new call to arms. The Zealots were certain that the moment of truth had arrived, and they tried to start an all-out Jewish revolt. Rebellious violence spread outside the city of Jerusalem. In the remote Judean desert to the south, a Roman garrison was stationed on the hilltop fortress of Masada. A band of Zealots assaulted the fortress stronghold and killed the entire Roman force, taking possession of the militarized mountain.

Driven by their passionate hatred for the Romans, the Jews had thrown caution aside and decided to fight their oppressors. Historian Martin Noth provided an assessment of the significance of these actions that would become known as the Great Jewish Revolt:

> The rebels were now masters of the situation. . . . They had succeeded in overcoming the Herodian fortress of Masada on the Dead Sea, and in Jerusalem they decided to stop the daily sacrifices for the emperor and not to accept any further sacrifices from foreigners. This meant a complete break with the Roman power, going far beyond the various lesser or more serious conflicts in the country, and all that remained now was a struggle to the death.

Once the Jewish people, led by groups such as the Zealots, began to stand their ground against Roman authority in their kingdom, especially in Jerusalem, there was no turning back. The revolt gained momentum and spread rapidly. The Sicarii joined the Zealots, and attacks on Roman positions around the city began to occur regularly.

For many Jews, the garrison fortress located next to the Temple, the Antonia, was a major symbol of Roman oppression. The fortress had been built to help Roman soldiers keep a watchful eye on Jewish activities inside the Temple courtyard and on the Temple platform, where crowds gathered for holy days and feast days. The fortress stood taller than the Temple, allowing the Romans a constant view. In fact, the Antonia was dominated by a watchtower. When thousands of Jews gathered in the Temple platform area, as they did during Passover, Roman troops were placed along the tops of the Antonia's porticoes, ready for trouble as they kept tabs on the crowd below.

In August, the Zealots and other rebels attacked the Antonia and besieged the hated military post. After a two-day siege, the Jews broke into the Antonia and massacred the entire Roman garrison in a powerful act of defiance. The Jews then burned down the Antonia.

Other Roman forces in the city took refuge in three large towers that had been built by Herod the Great. This left the king's palace undefended. The historian Josephus wrote that "They [the Jewish rebels] put the king's palace to the torch and burned down the public archives, thus winning over the poor and impoverished, whose records of debts had gone up in flames." Then, the Zealots attacked pro-Roman residents who had hidden in the king's palace.

The Jewish takeover of the Roman garrison at Masada played a key role in the events unfolding in the streets of Jerusalem. One of the Zealot leaders, Menahem, went to Masada with some of his men and collected badly needed weapons for the rebels in Jerusalem. When they entered the city with these arms, Menahem was hailed as a hero and put in command of the rebel forces. When he tried to don royal robes, however, in the hope that the Jews would make him

The Jews of Jerusalem considered the Antonia fortress, located beside the Temple, a symbol of their harsh treatment at the hands of the Romans. The tall fortress, in fact, overlooked the grounds of the Temple and was used by the Romans to keep a watch on the activities of the Jews. This is a scale model of the Antonia fortress in Jerusalem.

their new king, they turned on him, showering him with stones until he had to try to leave Jerusalem altogether. His rivals caught up with him before he could flee and put him to death. After this assassination of a Zealot leader, one of Menahem's colleagues, Eleazar, felt the pressure to leave the city. He went back to Masada.

The city of Jerusalem and the surrounding countryside were in full revolt. Towns around Judea were destroyed. Non-Jews—including Syrians, Samarians, and Greeks in Alexandria—were attacked by Jewish rebels. To stop the bloody violence, Cestius Gallus, the Syrian governor, marched his forces south. Already the Jewish revolt had cost thousands of lives. In Caesaria, according to Josephus, "the people [of the city] massacred the Jewish population. . . . More than twenty thousand Jews were slaughtered in less than an hour." In Alexandria, Josephus wrote, Roman legions killed 50,000 Jews.

After he occupied and established supply lines at Caesarea and Joppa, Gallus marched into Galilee with his forces, intending to teach the Jerusalem Jews, as well as Zealots and rebels throughout the kingdom, a powerful lesson. He reached the neighboring Jewish settlements around the great old city, taking prisoners and burning buildings. When the weather turned cold, however, he was forced to turn back, unable to lay siege to Jerusalem.

The Jewish fighters carried out decisive and offensive attacks as the Romans retreated. Historian Peter Connolly described the relentlessness of the Jewish assaults on the Romans:

> Swarming through the hills they attacked the retreating column at every opportunity. Whilst on open ground the Romans were able to beat off the attacks. When they began the descent along the hills towards Beth Horon the Jews launched an all-out attack on the baggage train driving it down into the valley. The main part of the Roman army managed to escape during the night but they were forced to abandon the baggage train with all their siege equipment. The Jews pursued the retreating column all the way to the coastal plain where the Romans could have brought their cavalry into play. The Jews called off the pursuit and returned to Jerusalem in triumph dragging the siege weapons with them.

When the retreat was over, the Romans counted their losses at more than 5,000 infantry soldiers and nearly 500 cavalry. The Jews, especially extremists such as the Zealots and Sicarii, were ecstatic that they had removed the power of Rome from their lands. With each victory for the rebellious Jews, however, the Roman Empire became more resolved not only to bring the revolt to an end, but to crush it completely.

Having escaped Jerusalem with some of his men, Gallus wrote a dispatch to Greece for Emperor Nero. The next spring, in A.D. 67, Nero sent one of his most seasoned generals to Judea with a gigantic army. The general was Vespasian, a field commander with more than 20 years of experience. Then in his late fifties, Vespasian had conquered forces in Britain. His son, Titus, was one of his commanders.

Vespasian's march was ruthless. Fearing his advance, some towns simply surrendered without a fight. Field armies of Jews fled in the face of the approaching Roman armies that intended to destroy the rebels. Towns were captured and burned. Prisoners were taken and forced into slavery. When Vespasian conquered the Jewish city of Gabara in Upper Galilee, he ordered the execution of all adult males and then set the city ablaze.

As they continued toward Jerusalem, the Romans laid waste to the countryside. Meanwhile, in Jerusalem, the various groups involved in the revolt were not in agreement. The extremists—the Zealots and the Sicarii—wanted to fight to the death. Other groups in the city were not as eager to die. They hoped a peaceful solution could be found to settle problems between the Jews and the Romans. After the Roman authorities left Jerusalem, most of the people did not want the Zealots to take the leadership of the city. They looked instead to the same Jewish leaders who had cooperated with the Romans.

Much of the history of the Jewish revolt comes through

Roman General Vespasian was sent by Emperor Nero to deal with the Jewish revolt in A.D. 67. Vespasian was brutal in his treatment of the Jews as he defeated the rebels in several confrontations.

the writings of the great Jewish historian, Josephus. He was not only a witness to the events of the war, but he also took part in the military activities as a commander of Galilean troops. Josephus soon proved to be a better historian than military leader. He was not able to unite the Galileans against the Romans. In the face of Vespasian's advancing troops, the Galileans deserted east to the city of Tiberias, along the Sea of Galilee. Josephus then moved on to a mountain town, Jotapata, hoping to gather a force to harass Roman supply lines. Vespasian, however, was aware of the military unit in Jotapata. He soon surrounded the city and began a huge siege designed to bring about the collapse of the Galilean town. The siege of the Romans against this Jewish community was, in some ways, a dress rehearsal for the siege of Masada that would take place five years later.

The Siege
of Jotapata

The Romans were the world's experts at siege warfare at the time of the Jewish revolt. They had many effective weapons, including battering rams, like the one seen in this relief sculpture from the eighth century B.C. The battering ram would slam into a city's walls until they gave way and allowed Roman troops to storm the fortress.

The Romans stood at the gates of Jotapata as Jewish rebels prepared to make a stand. The siege would last from June to July A.D. 67. The Jewish record of the siege, produced by Josephus, gave a fairly detailed description of the activities in which the Romans engaged in order to bring about the collapse of the armed rebels hidden behind the formidable walled fortifications of Jotapata.

Although Jotapata was a difficult position for the Romans to attack (the city could only be approached from an adjacent hilltop), the Roman forces were the ancient world's experts in siege warfare. Vespasian met with his war council to plan the siege against the Jewish fortifications. They determined that they would build a ramp leading to the wall of the fortress. The general ordered his men to scatter throughout the countryside to collect the materials they would need to create a huge ramp. The Romans felled many trees, piling up timber in huge stacks. They also piled up an enormous mountain of rocks. Then they began to build the ramp, using both stones and tree trunks. Many hundreds of soldiers worked on the ramp, stacking up the layers and filling the gaps with basketfuls of earth.

The work of the Roman troops was complicated by the Jewish defenders inside Jotapata. The rebels manned the citadel walls and tossed down stones and arrows and anything else they could find toward the approaching Romans. To ease the damage caused by these projectiles, the Romans built wooden sheds to protect themselves. These shelters were about eight feet long and were placed end to end to cover the ramp workers completely. The Jews lobbed their largest stones at the Roman shelters, yet many of the sheds withstood the attacks.

Then, Vespasian ordered his artillery to the front. Some 160 siege machines, including catapults, ballistas, and onagers (a variation on the catapult), were positioned to fire a variety of missiles down on the Jewish defenders. Each machine was designed to be able to lob anything—from a heavy stone to an iron-tipped javelin to a flaming pot of burning liquid—at the enemy. Once the entire battery of Roman artillery was loaded and ready to attack, Vespasian gave the order. The sky was filled with scores of projectiles aimed at the Jewish defenders in Jotapata.

As the Romans inched their way closer to the fortress walls, the Jewish rebels began to launch attacks of their own. Small, well-armed bands of defenders rushed out from the protective walls and raided the

Roman Siegecraft

Even before the first century A.D., the Romans were known for their expertise in besieging an apparently impregnable defensive position, such as the fortress at Jotapata. The earliest Roman siege known in history took place in Sicily 300 years before the siege at Jotapata.

In a typical Roman siege, the goal was to bring about the surrender of those defending the fortified position. Generally, this required a ramp to be built, which would allow the Romans to move up siege machines, such as battering rams, that were used to weaken the defensive walls. The ramp provided a smooth, gradual incline for the heavy machines.

A Roman battering ram usually had a long, wooden beam suspended from inside a mobile shelter, called a "tortoise." The outer portion of such a shelter was covered with "green wicker and layers of hide padded with seaweed or wet straw as a protection against bombardment." This shelter held the ram in place, and also provided cover for the soldiers manning the ram.

The Romans also relied on siege towers. These war machines stood tall enough to provide a raised platform that Roman archers could use to launch an attack or to hold some type of artillery weapon. Sometimes, the Romans made siege towers and battering ram shelters part of the same war machine.

The Romans had several types of artillery that could easily be used in a siege, since they could protect soldiers who were building a ramp or otherwise putting themselves within range of enemy projectiles. One type of artillery was the catapult. The Romans used two types of catapult, one that fired arrows (catapultae) and a second that launched stones (ballistae). In design, they were similar to the crossbows used in warfare during the Middle Ages, but they were larger in size. They drew the tension they needed to fire missiles from giant bands of twisted hair or sinew. The power of these bands was so great that it took several men to winch the "bowstring" back in place. Such hand-powered machines included a "slider," a center trough or guide where the missile was placed before launching. The bowstring was released with a trigger mechanism. The size of such engines varied widely, smaller varieties launched 6-foot-long (2-meter-long) spears to larger machines that lobbed 100-pound (45-kilogram) stones.

With such elaborate machinery, engineering skills, and hard-core determination, the Roman army rarely failed to bring down an enemy trapped inside a fortification. Once they isolated and surrounded their victims with a line of fortifications called a "circumvalation," the Romans had one of the most important weapons at their disposal, one that often determined a siege's outcome—time.

Romans who were building the ramp. The Jews killed their enemies and set fire to the shelters, then raced back to safety before the Roman commanders could respond. Despite their efforts, the work on the ramp went on.

Slowly and doggedly, the Roman troops brought their ramp closer and higher, until it was as high as the ramparts along the fortress wall. In desperation, the Jews found a way to answer the threat. Wooden palisades were placed along the wall, covered with wet animal hides to shield the wall above the ramp from the view of the Roman invaders. The sound of construction could be heard behind the temporary curtain. Josephus described the new strategy: "I summoned all the town's stonemasons and, protected by ingenious shields of ox hides, they raised the walls to a height of thirty feet." Once they completed their work, the Jews had made the wall in front of the ramp higher. The Roman building project now faced a significant setback.

Discouraged but not defeated, the Romans altered their strategy. Vespasian settled in for a longer siege, hoping to starve out the Jews or, perhaps, cause them to run short of water and die of thirst. Water had been rationed during the siege, so the Roman plan presented a real threat to the Jewish defenders. Josephus wrote that he met the challenge by tricking the Romans: "[To] deceive the Romans, I ordered dripping garments to be hung all around the battlements, as though water was so plentiful that we could afford to waste it. Then Vespasian gave up hope of starving the city and returned to the attack." At the same time, the Jews began to send men out of the fortress at night to gather food and water. The men crawled on all fours and wore animal skins. Roman sentries mistook the creeping Jews for stray dogs or herds of sheep.

By day, the Jews continued to raid the Roman camps outside the fortress walls. Vespasian put his men back to work on the ramp, certain that this was the best way to bring down the defenders at Jotapata. As the days passed, the Romans finally came close enough to the wall to be able to pound it with a battering ram, in the hope that they could cause the defense structure to collapse. Hidden within a large shelter like those the ramp builders used while they worked, the Romans' great battering ram, tipped in a heavy sheath of iron, performed its destructive work. To soften the blows of the ram, the Jews used ropes to lower sacks filled with straw down the walls. The trick worked, but the Romans soon began to use scythes (blades) attached to long poles to cut the ropes and get rid of the straw sacks.

Realizing the situation was bleak, large bands of Jewish warriors left the fortress to fight the Romans on the ramp. At first, they caught the Romans by surprise. They were able to set fire to the Roman shelters and many of the catapults, and also destroyed the battering ram. The Romans quickly recovered, however, and remounted the attack. They brought up another battering ram and went back to work, as the wall began to crack. Joining those who manned the ram were archers and slingmen. More siege machines also launched missiles of iron and stone toward the desperate defenders of the wall. The ram's assault—an endless pounding—continued. Archers fired their arrows without restraint. From their positions along the ramparts, the Jews fought back, firing down on the Romans below. The casualties on both sides

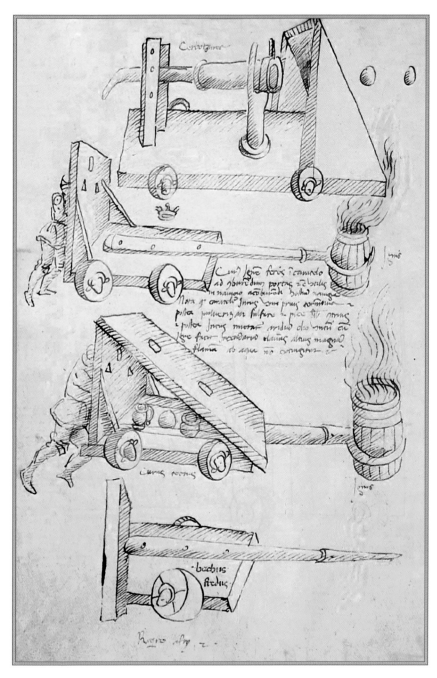

Among the Romans' siege weapons were catapults. These tools were used to launch many types of projectiles. Some of the most dangerous catapults hurled fire at the enemy.

mounted rapidly into the hundreds. Then, the following morning:

> The wall gave way just before daybreak. Stones cracked
> and were jarred loose. A parapet shuddered and then
> collapsed outward in an avalanche of wood and stone.
> When the dust settled, everyone could see that the wall
> had an opening wide enough for several men to enter
> side by side. The Jewish defenders rushed to close the
> breach . . . but they knew that time was running out for
> them. . . . The Romans knew it too. . . . At dawn,
> Vespasian gave the order to attack. All the trumpets of
> the army sounded at once in a mighty blast. At the same
> time all the troops gave a great shout, and all the bow-
> men let fly with so many arrows they darkened the sky.

The Jews did not wait for the Romans to enter without
a fight. They stormed out to meet their enemy, armed with
an array of swords, spears, and daggers. Jewish rebels also
continued to man the ramparts, throwing stones and firing
arrows at the Roman invaders. The ferocity of the assault
reached a feverish pitch as the Jewish counterattack sent the
Romans into retreat. This turned out to be only a reprieve.
Roman reserve troops joined the assault, breathing new life
in the attack.

As the Romans moved up their assault ramp for a
second time, the Jews tried new strategies. According to the
record written by Josephus:

> Hand-to-hand fighting ensued. The Romans formed a
> solid roof of shields and pushed the Jewish defenders up
> to the wall. I ordered boiling oil poured on these close-
> locked shields and broke up the formation. We poured
> slippery herbs on the Roman bridges and gangways, and
> the troops lost footing and were crushed.

The oil and the slippery vegetable mass left the ramp and the gangways slick, making it difficult for the Romans to continue the assault without sliding into one another, falling, or otherwise making themselves easy targets for skilled Jewish archers. Vespasian broke off the attack and the Jews immediately began to repair the breach in their defensive wall.

Still, this ferocious attack by the Romans marked the approaching end for the Jews. The defenders were running out of options, as well as resources, including oil, water, and spirit. Despite the tenacity of the Jews at Jotapata, in the end, two facts could not be ignored: The city walls had been breached and the Romans were superior in number.

After the Jews had defended Jotapata for 47 days, the Romans finally took control of the city. The collapse of the Jewish stronghold came after Vespasian learned that some of the Jewish sentries, at a certain time of night, fell asleep at their posts, exhausted from fighting. Vespasian sent troops quietly to the wall. They scaled it quickly and killed the guards on the ramparts. Josephus provided the details of the final day of the siege:

> When day broke, the citadel had already been captured and the enemy soldiers were spreading everywhere within it. But the inhabitants were unaware of what had happened; worn out by fatigue, most of them still slept. Those who were awake found that a dense morning mist covered everything, making it difficult to see. Not until the whole Roman army had poured in did they realize what had happened— and then it was too late. Jotapata had fallen, and death was at their throats. The Romans, remembering

all the trouble they had been caused during the siege, were merciless to the Jews. They slaughtered them, throwing their bodies down the mountainsides. . . . The Romans carried 1,200 prisoners off into slavery. The total number of Jews they killed came to 40,000. . . . Thus ended the siege of Jotapata.

Although the Romans carried out a massacre against the Jewish defenders in Jotapata, Josephus, the garrison commander, was able to escape. As the Romans spread through the city, killing almost everyone, Josephus and 40 others, mostly people of rank and importance, hid in a cave. For three days, they were able to remain safe. According to his written record of the events, Josephus "ventured forth [at night] looking for a way to escape." Finally, a female prisoner told the Romans where Josephus was hiding. Vespasian then sent a Jewish messenger to Josephus, informing him that his life would be spared if he surrendered. Josephus agreed. His comrades, however, would not allow him to leave the cave. As he put it, they "threatened me if I made a move to surrender to . . . the Romans. . . . They pointed their swords at me and threatened to run me through."

His companions chose to commit a mass suicide, rather than have any of them surrender. Josephus agreed to take part. Each member of the group committed suicide, leaving Josephus the last one still alive. He then surrendered to the Romans, just as he had intended in the first place. As he had promised, Vespasian was lenient with Josephus. He not only allowed the commander to live, but took him into Roman headquarters. In time, Josephus won the favor of Vespasian, who granted Josephus his freedom. Circumstances worked out well

When the siege of Jotapata ended, the survivors fled and hid out in a cave. Rather than give in to the Roman conquerors, they chose to commit mass suicide. Only one person did not take part in the suicide — Josephus, who surrendered to the Romans, as depicted in this painting in a French manuscript from the last quarter of the fifteenth century. He became a leading historian who chronicled the Jewish revolt.

for Josephus. Vespasian became the Roman emperor two years later. The defeated Jewish commander later settled in Rome. There, he became a favorite of Vespasian's two sons, Titus and Domitian, both of whom followed their father as emperor. Back in Judea, however, many Jews considered Josephus a traitor.

Destruction
in Jerusalem

When they defeated the defenders of Jerusalem, the Roman army entered the city and destroyed valuable property as well as treasured religious relics. This fifteenth-century Italian painting by Ercole de' Roberti depicts the destruction.

ollowing the victory at Jotapata, Vespasian rested his army before marching on another Jewish city, Tiberias, near the Sea of Galilee to the east. In the aftermath of Jotapata, however, the people of Tiberias chose to surrender without a fight. The city of Taricheae was Vespasian's next target. The Jews there attempted to make a stand against Vespasian's troops, but the Romans stormed the city. When a large number of Jews tried to escape in boats, the Romans built their own rafts, which allowed Roman archers to cut down the escapees, whose bodies were left floating in the waters of the Sea of Galilee.

63

Seeing the fate of Taricheae, other cities in the region surrendered quickly. A few tried to fight, though, such as the town of Gamala. There, the Romans managed to undermine a wall tower under cover of darkness. When the tower fell, the Romans poured into the city and killed everyone inside, except for two women. Many of the city's residents killed themselves by leaping off the defensive citadel. In a short time, Galilee had been lost to the Romans.

By early spring of A.D. 68, Vespasian sent his forces against several Jewish communities in the region of Peraea, located northeast of the Sea of Galilee. Here, many rebels were killed, the village stormed, the population massacred, and the town set ablaze. As Vespasian's army carried out its harsh destruction of Judea and the surrounding lands, the city of Jerusalem was slowly cut off from the outside world. Both Jews and Romans understood that Jerusalem was the ultimate goal of the Roman march.

In the fall of A.D. 68, Roman Emperor Nero died suddenly. A new emperor, Galba, the governor of Spain, took the Roman throne. Vespasian sent one of his sons, Titus, to Rome to pay respects to the new ruler. However, while passing through Greece, Titus received word that Galba had been murdered. Over the next year, the future of the Roman throne seemed to be unsettled. From A.D. 68 until the summer of A.D. 69, Vespasian did little in the field. He stayed in place, waiting for clear orders from a new emperor. As pro-Jewish forces gained strength, though, the Roman general decided that he had to act.

Vespasian moved south toward the city of Jerusalem, defeating hold-out cities such as Gophna to the north, and cutting off access to key roads. Then he invaded Idumaea, the homeland of the former king of Judea,

Herod the Great. The city of Hebron, south of Jerusalem, was subdued, which left only a few fortresses in the region—including Herodium, Machaerus, and Herod's old palace grounds at Masada—still standing.

As the Romans boxed in the city of Jerusalem, the Jews within its protective walls engaged in a power struggle of their own. The Zealots and anti-Zealots were fighting for control of the city. This left Jerusalem extremely vulnerable to attack, since the forces inside the city were unable to come to terms and decide on a plan to face the advancing Roman army.

As Jerusalem was racked by division, however, so was the Roman Empire. Various Roman leaders, including generals, all vied to become emperor. In the midst of the power struggle, Vespasian determined to make his own play for control of the empire. On July 1, A.D. 69, much of the eastern half of the Roman Empire declared its support for the general. In just a few months, Vespasian emerged as the new emperor. He turned his Jewish revolt campaign over to his son, Titus, and sailed to Rome.

By fall, it was too late to launch an extensive campaign against Jerusalem, so Titus waited about one mile (1.6 kilometers) outside the city, in the area known as the Mount of Olives, where Jesus Christ had prayed the night before being crucified. Inside the city, two rival Zealot factions were involved in a heated power struggle. Josephus described the impact of this political infighting: "I maintain that it was the internal strife that overthrew the city, and I say that all the tragedy that befell the city may be blamed on her own people." The rivalries led the factions to destroy each other's food supplies, depots of grain that had been stored in anticipation of a possible Roman siege.

The next spring, the Romans prepared to attack.

Titus struck at the city with large catapults, which reached the Temple grounds, while Roman engineers and infantry-men began to build a ramp on the opposite side of Jerusalem. Once the siege began, the rival bands of Jews in the city shook off their differences and united to defend Jerusalem.

Many of the events of the siege of Jerusalem were similar to what had occurred in earlier Roman sieges of Judean strongholds, including Jotapata. As the Romans built their ramp, Jewish defenders fought from the ramparts along the city walls, hurling down firebrands to ignite the Roman siege machines and shelters. The number of Jewish warriors defending the city was between 20,000 and 25,000. Bands of fighters came out from the city walls to slow the Romans' progress on the ramp. Because the Romans approached from several sides of the city walls, it proved to be difficult for the Jews to stop the Roman advance. Unlike the siege at Jotapata, during which the Romans had been forced to erect a massive ramp toward the city walls, at Jerusalem, Titus spent the winter of 69–70 preparing the ground outside Jerusalem's walls for the siege. Historian Josephus described the groundwork Titus and his troops accomplished before the siege began in the spring:

> Titus . . . ordered his main army to level all the inter-vening ground right up to the walls. Every fence and hedge was swept away, every fruit tree within the area felled. The hollows in the terrain were filled up, the jutting rocks smoothed with iron tools, and the whole space between Scopus and Herod's monuments . . . was flattened out to a dead level.

This preliminary work helped keep the Romans' ramp-building to a minimum.

As battering rams were brought up, Titus was kept busy repelling Jewish fighters, as well as flaming missiles. Once the battering rams began to pound the city's walls, the Romans started to count the days until victory. At the same time, another consideration was also probably on the minds of both the Romans and the Jews. According to ancient tradition, once a battering ram dealt its first blow to an enemy's wall, it meant that the ultimate surrender would have to be unconditional.

Although the Jews continued to harass the besieging Romans, the battering rams continued their work, too. By the fifteenth day of the siege, one of the rams, which had been named "Victor," destroyed part of the Jerusalem wall, causing it to collapse. Although the Jews retreated behind a second, interior wall in a different section of the city, within five days, this wall had been breached as well. This left the Temple grounds and the Antonia fortress open to attack. To make matters worse, within the city, people were beginning to run out of food and some were beginning to starve. Despite their clear advantage, the Romans took a break, spending most of a week paying their troops, and making the Jews wait for their final destruction.

Once the battle commenced again, the Jews were as defiant as ever. During this phase of the assault, Titus ordered Josephus, who was present during the siege, to try to talk his fellow Jews out of continuing their resistance. It would be difficult work for Josephus. He wrote about his experience:

> [Titus] delegated me, Josephus, to parley with the defenders in our native tongue, thinking that they might yield more readily to the persuasions of a fellow-countryman. Accordingly, I Josephus, went round the walls, keeping well out of range of the

Jewish artillerymen but still within hearing distance. I repeatedly implored them to spare themselves and the people, their country and their Temple. During my appeals I was derided by many from the ramparts and reviled by others. . . . But, despite my . . . strong appeals, the insurgents would not budge from their doomed course. . . . Some people, however, were incited to desert.

As Titus moved his men deeper into the heart of the city of Jerusalem, he had a circumvalation erected around the city. Stretching nearly 5 miles (8 kilometers), it was intended to ensure that no one would escape. Roman troops built 13 watchtowers along the perimeter ring.

Meanwhile, starvation was causing the Jews to turn on one another. Hundreds were dying each day. Desperate people raided one another's homes in search of food. Famine began to claim more lives than the Romans did. As the city's poorer people came outside the Jerusalem walls to look for food, they were captured, flogged, and hung on crosses. Sometimes hundreds were crucified at a time. Some wealthier Jews swallowed their money before they left the city, so that the Romans could not steal it from them. According to historian Peter Connolly: "When one of these was caught retrieving his money the soldiers went berserk. Rumor spread that the deserters were full of gold and many were ripped open and their bowels searched."

Once inside the city, Titus ordered his men to erect a ramp toward the old Roman garrison post, the Antonia. The ramp-building took 17 days to finish. The Zealots in the city hatched a construction project of their own to meet the challenge of the ramp. They dug beneath the Temple platform, directly below the ramp, holding up their tunnel with wooden beams. When they completed their

Despite infighting among the rebel factions, the Jews of Jerusalem put up a fierce resistance to Titus and his troops, shown in this sixteenth-century Italian tapestry.

underground trap, they set fire to the beams. The resulting collapse caused the ramp to cave into the subterranean breach. Then, the logs used in building the ramp caught fire, destroying the entire engineering project. The Romans were not daunted, however. A new ramp was ready within three weeks. Jewish attempts to burn this ramp failed.

Then, to the excitement of the Romans, the tunnel that the Zealots had dug under the wall to collapse the Roman ramp caused the wall itself to topple over. The Zealots had anticipated this, though, and had built another wall behind the Antonia wall. Even so, within a few days, the Romans quietly scaled the Temple wall and killed the Jewish guards. Once they were inside, a Roman trumpeter blasted the call to arms, throwing the Jews in the city into a panic. In short order, Roman soldiers and Zealots were fighting on the Temple platform. The tenacity of the Zealots pushed the Romans back inside the Antonia.

Once inside, the Romans began to take apart the old Herodian fortress, reducing it down to ground level so that Titus could extend his ramp directly to the Temple platform. Once this ramp was completed, it provided a causeway wide enough to let large numbers of troops, including cavalry, enter the Temple grounds. Driven by a desire to make the Jews who had dared to defy the power of Rome pay a high price for their actions, Titus ordered the Temple grounds to be torched.

As the Temple grounds burned, Titus and his men entered the sacred Temple and desecrated the Jewish religious center by sacrificing an ox, a sheep, and a pig. Not only were they committing sacrilege against the Judaic faith by their very presence in the Temple, but the Jews considered a pig an unclean animal. To sacrifice the animal was a final insult.

As Zealot resistance fell apart, the Jewish rebel leaders tried to negotiate with the Romans for better terms of surrender. However, Titus would accept nothing less than an unconditional surrender. Some holdouts barricaded themselves in the Upper City, and the Romans had to build new ramps and start the process all over again.

Archaeology Reveals the Destruction of Jerusalem

As the Romans set out to destroy the city of Jerusalem, they left the urban landscape an utter wasteland. As the historian Josephus described the destruction, the city was "so completely leveled to the ground as to leave future visitors no reason for believing that the place had ever been inhabited."

For centuries, much information about what the ancient buildings looked like, as well as where exactly they were located, was a mystery. Eventually, many years later, especially after 1967, when Israel captured Jerusalem in the Six-Day War, archaeologists unearthed much of the grounds where the important buildings had once stood. Among the sites they found were the location of the Antonia and the various Temple grounds. A clearer picture has since emerged. Sometimes, however, the view archaeologists have discovered has not agreed with the written record, including that of Josephus.

These excavations have helped archaeologists learn more about the places that were so significant in the Great Jewish Revolt. Archaeological studies have also shown just how huge Herod the Great's building projects were.

The entire area around the southern end of the Temple platform has been unearthed. Excavations have also been carried out in the old Jewish quarter of the city and the Upper City, where the last of the Zealots held out against the Romans. Through such excavations, archaeologists have found many signs of the Roman destruction. Nearly all the houses beneath the Jewish quarter show signs of having been burned. Many weapons, both Jewish and Roman, have been dug up and are now preserved. Occasionally, archaeologists have unearthed human skeletal remains that show the person died a violent death.

Digging has revealed many signs of Roman destruction to the south of the Temple platform as well. Ruins of a Jewish meeting hall have been found, thrown down at the southern end of the platform. Archaeologists have also dug up columns, which were found in a scattered, collapsed state.

Although modern archaeology has given today's scholars a better picture of Jerusalem's history and construction, no archaeological dig has been made on the Temple site itself. Today, that ground is considered an Islamic holy site, where no digs may be carried out.

When he entered Jerusalem, Titus ordered his troops to burn down the Temple. As the flames destroyed the Temple grounds, the Roman troops went inside the Temple itself and desecrated the sacred house of worship. This scene was rendered by an eighteenth-century Italian historical painter, Francesco Hayez.

Within a few more weeks, the siege of Jerusalem was over. The ancient Hebrew city, one that had witnessed more than 1,000 years of Jewish history, was subjected to unspeakable terrors at the hands of the Romans:

Masses of prisoners were rounded up. The old and the ill were killed off and the remainder confined in the court of the women on the Temple platform. All the Zealots and their supporters were separated and executed. The 700 tallest and most handsome of the prisoners were reserved for the triumph. The rest were sent to the amphitheatres of the east where during the autumn of 70 A.D. they were killed for sport. Some were killed in combats, some by wild beasts and others were burned alive. Jerusalem was now systematically destroyed. The walls flattened. The Temple and its platform were broken up. Only the three massive towers . . . that had been built by Herod . . . were left standing.

As horrific as the destruction of ancient property was psychologically to the Jews in Jerusalem, the defeat also had a huge human cost. Hundreds of thousands of people lost their lives. Josephus described the terrible fate of the people of Jerusalem:

No pity was shown for age, no reverence for rank. Children and graybeards, laity and priests, all were massacred. The roar of the flames mingled with the groans of the falling victims. The din was deafening. The war cries of the Roman legions, sweeping onward in a mass, mixed with the howls of the rebels, encircled by fire and sword, and the shrieks of the people, fleeing panic-stricken into the arms of their enemies. . . . Out of all that multitude not a soul escaped.

Some did escape, however, using the various tunnels that had been dug beneath the city walls. Among them was a Zealot captain named Eleazar Ben Ya'ir, who would play such an important role two years later during the siege of Masada. From there, the survivors of Jerusalem took to the hills, scattering throughout Judea, to escape the harsh punishment of the victorious Romans. One group of Zealots reached the mountaintop stronghold at Masada, one of only three Jewish fortress positions that had not yet fallen into Roman hands.

The two main leaders of the Zealots who had defended Jerusalem, Simon Bar Giora and John of Gischala, did not escape. After "Jerusalem was reduced to a smoldering heap of rubble" Titus returned with his captives and spoils of war to Rome, where he was honored by a triumphal parade to show the Roman people the great deeds their generals in the field had achieved. Titus watched the processional alongside his father, Emperor Vespasian. Among those items on display during the parade were the treasures of distant lands, such as Judea. Romans carried artifacts stolen from the Jewish Holy Temple, including a "great golden table, a colossal seven-branched menorah, and several sacred Torah scrolls." After these trophies of conquest passed by came long human chains of Jewish captives, including the Zealot leader, Simon Bar Giora. Writer Neil Waldman described the scene:

> A group of Roman guards approached Simon Bar Giora, who had been marching at the head of the Jewish prisoners. They bound his hands behind his back and placed a noose around his neck. A centurion on horseback took the rope and began pulling him through the streets. At first, he ran behind the prancing horse, but soon the horse began to gallop. Simon lost his balance and fell. He twisted and bounced on the cobblestones as the centurion dragged him onward, slowly choking him to death. His limp and broken body was brought to the spot on the Forum reserved for those who had committed crimes against the state.

With Titus back in Rome, the campaign to conquer Judea was left unfinished. A new Roman governor, Lucillus Bassus, was sent to destroy the last of the Jewish rebellion in Judea. Bassus managed to capture the defensive fortress at Herodium, the site where Herod the Great was buried. Then, he marched to the stronghold at Machaerus, a rocky hill of "immense height and surrounded on all sides by deep ravines." Bassus's campaign was cut short when he died suddenly. Flavius Silva was chosen to take his place. Only one rebellious holdout remained to be conquered by the Romans, the Herodian fortress nestled atop a pillar of desert rock—Masada.

Centuries after the fall of Masada, archaeologists have uncovered many items used during the historic siege, including these stone balls, which would have been launched by catapults.

The Last Stronghold

Everyone in Judea understood the importance of the Zealot stronghold at Masada after the collapse of Machaerus and Herodium. The Romans had conquered the land, its farms and estates, as well as its important cities, including the ancient capital of Jerusalem. Only one significant holdout of Zealot resolve still stood defiantly—the windswept mountain plateau of Masada. Two years had passed since the collapse, destruction, and desolation of Jerusalem. Rome could now concentrate its entire strength on this fortress by the sea.

General Flavius Silva was a hardened Roman warrior. He would not be lenient with those who were now poised to defy the authority of the Roman Empire. The Jewish historian Josephus left a record of the symbolism of the fight that was approaching: "Now that the entire land had been conquered except for this single fortress, Silva brought together all the troops under his command and marched against it." Despite his superior forces, Silva would find Masada difficult to subdue.

Between the fall of Jerusalem in A.D. 70 and the beginning of the great Roman siege at Masada, many refugees from the Roman campaigns had hidden out in the Judean desert, in caves, and in other remote sanctuaries until they could no longer find food or security. Those who arrived at the Dead Sea fortress were often hungry and thirsty, desperate to find shelter and fellow Jews who still intended to fight the Romans. By the time the siege began in the fall of A.D. 72, Masada was home to nearly 1,000 people, mostly Zealots and their families.

The Zealots of Masada, many of whom were Sicarii, had found everything they could possibly ask for to withstand a lengthy siege. By taking over the extensive palace systems, as well as storage buildings, baths, and other buildings, the Zealots had plenty of rooms to house themselves, as well as plenty of food. Josephus described how Herod's work on Masada paid off well for the Zealots so many years later:

> The interior of the palace—its living quarters, colonnades, and baths—was richly furnished, with much variety. At every spot used for living purposes, both on the summit and around the palace, Herod had cut out in the rock numerous large cisterns as reservoirs for water, thus making it possible to put in an ample supply. . . . In addition, the stores inside the fortress were amazing because of their lavishness and splendor as well as for their state of preservation. For here had been stored a

huge supply of [grain], amply sufficient to last for years, abundance of wine and oil, besides every variety of seeds and piles of dates. These were found in perfect condition, as fresh and as good as the day they were first put in a hundred years earlier. It would not be incorrect to attribute the preservation to the high altitude of the plateau.

Just as important to help them defend Masada against a protracted siege, the Zealots found a large supply of "arms of every description, stored there by Herod and sufficient for ten thousand men."

During the two years after the fall of Jerusalem, those who lived atop Masada tried to live as normally as possible. They studied Judaism and met three times a day in their hilltop synagogue to pray. A rabbi taught the men about the Torah, the sacred collection of Jewish writings. The Zealots chose Eleazar Ben Ya'ir to be their leader. Ben Ya'ir had been a captain during the Jewish rebellion. He was a strong leader who was greatly respected by his people.

Meanwhile, Silva prepared his army for a long siege by taking care of the usual military needs. Knowing that many of those who had taken refuge at Masada had escaped first from the fighting in Jerusalem, Silva did not intend to let these obstinate Jews escape for a second time. To that end, he ordered a circumvalation to be built around the base of the Masada outcropping. This restricting wall was enormous. It measured 2 miles (3 kilometers) in a full circle and was 6 feet (2 meters) thick in many places. As the Romans erected this structure, they created a gigantic human pen that included 12 towers. The Romans also set up eight encampments along this barrier wall. Two of the camps were quite large, while the remaining six were smaller. Among them they housed the entire Roman army under Silva's command. One of the encampments was Silva's. He carefully selected his own position on the field below Masada. The spot was a plateau of rock called White Promontory, because the whitish tint of the rock there reflected the brilliant sunlight. As Josephus described it, Silva "encamped at a spot where the fortress abutted on an adjacent mountain." Silva purposefully chose a site that was close to the occupied mountain and as high up on the cliff walls as he could get. The mountaintop was 1,300 feet (396 meters) at its greatest height, but White Promontory was only 400 feet (122 meters) from the top of Masada.

The military camps became organized communities, complete with streets and permanent tents to house the troops. Each tent complex held eight to nine soldiers. The Romans also built an officers' facility, where the Roman leaders could hold meetings and discuss strategy.

Between the wall and the base of the Masada outcropping, the Romans kept thousands of prisoner-slaves who had been captured during the Judean campaign. These workers had been brought along to provide labor for the Romans. The remains of both the Roman circumvalation and the camps can be seen from the air even today. The camps and the area enclosed by the siege wall became home to approximately 15,000 people, both Roman and non-Roman.

Having sealed off any possible way of escape, Silva then ordered the construction of a ramp to reach the summit of the mountain. Thousands of men—Roman soldiers and prisoners of war alike—began the monumental task. Silva's plan centered around the ramp he ordered built. Just as they had done at other sieges, the Romans would use their finished ramp to deliver a large siege tower and a battering ram to the top of the man-made incline. While the ramp was under construction, Roman artillerymen would use their siege machines to launch missiles, including large arrows, flaming pots of burning oil, and heavy stones, at the

General Silva made detailed preparations for the siege at Masada.
The camps he set up for his troops were huge and elaborate. The
ruins of these camps can still be seen from the air today.

Zealot positions. The Roman battering ram would then
cause destruction to the hilltop wall. Once part of the
perimeter wall atop the mountain stronghold collapsed,
Roman soldiers would stream up toward the Jewish
positions, bringing about their defeat.

Although the Romans understood the difficulties that
lay ahead of them, they could not have guessed how long it

would take to bring down this Jewish fortress. The Jotapata siege had lasted for a grueling seven weeks. This siege, the climax of the Roman campaign against rebellious Judea, would go on for about seven *months*.

Yet even as the Romans built confining walls at the base of Masada and got to work on their ramp, the Jewish defenders harassed them constantly. Their arrows reached their Roman targets, while huge rocks and boulders pounded down the mountainside, crashing into enemy positions below. Jewish warriors even slipped past Roman guards, entered Roman tents and killed Roman soldiers in their sleep.

Even as the ramp grew in size, despite Jewish harassment and attacks, Silva realized that the incline was not strong enough to bear the weight of great siege engines and battering rams. Josephus described the Roman leader's answer to the problem:

> [Silva] ordered his troops to throw up an earthen embankment, a solid bank, which they raised to the height of three hundred feet. But it was still not solid enough or big enough to hold the war engines. So on top of it was constructed a platform of great stones fitted closely together, seventy-five feet wide and just as long.

The siege machines Silva used at Masada were similar to those the Romans had used at other sieges in Judea by Vespasian and his son, Titus. One type was a siege tower that stood 90 feet (27 meters) high and was sheathed in iron. The Romans covered the tower with iron so it would not be set ablaze by the torches and firebrands launched by the Jews on the mountain. It was the immense weight of such engines that required the fortification of the Roman ramp.

All these efforts, both defensive and offensive, required months of work and organization. At last, the Romans were ready to raise the siege tower up the ramp. In his book

Masada, Neil Waldman described this effort and the feat of engineering needed to deliver the tower to the top of the newly constructed ramp:

> With huge pulleys, the slaves began hauling large cubes of rock up the long incline. Upon the top of the ramp, they constructed a square platform seventy-five feet wide. They then attached the massive assault tower to the pulleys and began hauling it up the ramp. Beneath the sting of roman whips, the slaves slowly dragged the huge tower into position and anchored it to the platform.

Even as the siege tower was hoisted up the ramp, the Romans also moved a huge battering ram into place to begin pounding at the base of the Masada wall. In Josephus's words, "With difficulty, [Silva] succeeded in effecting a breach and brought the wall, which guarded the summit, down in ruins."

The Jews were not immediately undone, however. Because the siege ramp, the tower, and the battering ram all approached the Masada walls from the same angle, the Zealots had prepared for the collapse of their defensive wall at that point by constructing another wall directly behind the section that would be brought down by the battering ram. The problem was that this newly constructed wall was not made of stone. Instead, it featured two attached walls of wooden beams with a space between them that was filled with dirt. Surprisingly, the wall made of wood and earth was able to withstand the pounding of the Roman battering ram better than the stone walls had. The dirt between the wooden walls served as a buffer, a cushion against the ram's blows. In fact, each strike from the battering ram helped pack the earthen wall tighter, making it even stronger.

Silva turned to another weapon, one he could not use

against the stone walls of Masada—fire. He ordered his men to "destroy this inner wall by fire. Since it was made mainly of wood, it quickly caught fire, blazing up in flames." Just as the flames licked at the wooden wall, however, the wind on the mountaintop shifted toward the Romans, changing the direction of the fire that threatened to engulf them and consume their siege engines. The Romans panicked. Then, in a complete turnabout, the wind shifted again, back in the direction of the already burning wall. Josephus described the change in the wind's direction as a sign from God that showed his disappointment with the Zealots.

Quickly, the searing heat and flames of the fire consumed the wooden wall, laying the fortress open for an attack. The fire kept the Romans from attacking at that very moment, though. Instead, they returned down the ramp, certain that they would achieve victory the following morning. Silva ordered all guards to be on their most alert watch to make certain not a single Jew escaped during the night.

The Zealots appeared to be trapped. Each of them faced an inevitable future. Dawn would bring the Romans, intent on the deaths of all male Zealot warriors, regardless of age. The women would be subjected to the usual Roman treatment: humiliation, possibly rape, and finally, slavery. The nearly 1,000 occupants of Masada had limited options. They could try to flee the mountaintop, but it would be impossible for everyone to escape. One misstep, one accidental sound from any one of them—a group that included children—and a mass escape attempt would be discovered by the Romans.

The Zealot commander, Eleazar Ben Ya'ir, faced the most important decision of his life: to continue to lead his people to their deaths against the Romans or to surrender his entire garrison and hope for charity from the Roman soldiers. But, in fact, Eleazar assembled his followers together and presented them with one other choice. Josephus provides the words of Ben Ya'ir in his book on the Jewish revolt. Speaking to the resistance fighters, Ben Ya'ir said:

> Long ago, my brave men, we resolved neither to serve the Romans nor any other except our God. . . . Now the time has come when we must test our resolution by our actions. At this crisis, let us not disgrace ourselves. . . . Let us not now accept slavery, with all the punishments awaiting us if we fall alive into Roman hands. . . . For as we were the first of all to revolt, so are we the last in arms against them. . . . I believe that it is God who has granted us this favor, that we have it in our power to die nobly and in freedom.

Ben Ya'ir continued to speak of honor, liberty, and the power of the enemy now waiting to take them captive or kill them. He spoke of God's wrath against them, the last members of the Jewish revolt. He asked, "Did we, in truth, really hope that we alone of all the Jewish nation would survive and preserve our freedom?" Then, Ben Ya'ir suggested a final solution that many were beginning to see as the most reasonable option—mass suicide:

> But let us not pay the penalty for our sins to our bitterest foes, the Romans, but rather to God Himself, through an act of our own hands. Let our wives die undishonored, our children with no knowledge of slavery. . . . But first let us destroy our possessions and the whole fortress by fire, for the Romans will be deeply chagrined to find neither our persons nor anything of value to loot. Let us spare only our food supply, for it will testify, when we are dead, that it was not want which subdued us, but that, as we resolved at the beginning of the war, we chose death, not slavery.

Even as Ben Ya'ir spoke, some of the Zealots were

already convinced that his proposal would bring the most honorable death for each of them. Others were not as certain. Still others began to weep and moan, terrified by this suggestion from their leader. Ben Ya'ir realized that he had not won over the entire community of Zealots. He then launched into a depiction of those who had fought Rome, lost, and had been taken prisoner. It was easy for the Zealots on Masada to picture the scenario. They had to look no further than the base of their mountain fortress, where thousands of Jewish prisoners of war were serving the Roman garrisons as slaves, forced to do the Romans' will, even helping bring death and destruction to their fellow Jews atop Masada. At the same time, Ben Ya'ir reminded his people of the destruction of their great and holy city, Jerusalem:

> But the multitudes now in Roman hands, who would not pity? Who would not rush to die rather than share their fate? . . . Most miserable of all are those still alive. How often have they prayed for death but it never comes! . . . Where now is that great city, the mother city of the Jews . . . defended by so many thousands of heroic men? . . . Her sole memorial are the dead still buried in her ruins . . . Only miserable old men sit beside the ashes of the shrine. Which of us, knowing this, could bear to behold the sun, even if he could live safely, free from peril? Who hates his country so much, who is so unmanly, so fond of life, that he is not sorry to be alive today? . . . We have been misled by an honorable hope that we might succeed . . . but now that hope has vanished. So let us hasten to die honorably. Let us have pity on ourselves, our children, and our wives, while we can. . . . Is a man to see his wife led off to violation, to hear the voice of his child crying "Father," when his own hands are bound? No, while those hands are free and can hold a sword, let us die as free men with our children and wives. Let us quit this life together!

Although he intended to continue his call for death and honor over humiliation and bondage, Ben Ya'ir did not need to speak another word. He had won over his followers. They were ready to commit themselves immediately to the mass suicide. Husbands and fathers gathered their families and hurriedly carried out the sad deeds. Josephus wrote: "They took their wives and children in their arms, clinging to them with tears and with parting kisses and caresses. At that instant, as though guided by other hands than their own, they performed their purpose. All carried the task through with their dearest ones." While the Romans below planned their assault on the Zealot stronghold for the following morning, the Jews on Masada were bringing an end to the siege in their own way.

Once the women and children had been killed, the men gathered up the belongings of the entire group, piled them together and set them to the torch. Then, the Zealot warriors drew lots and selected ten among them to kill all the others. After the ten were selected, each remaining Zealot lay down with his family, took them in his arms, and awaited his own death. Josephus said, "they offered their own throats to the sword." Just as the lives of their families had been ended quickly, so were the fathers and husbands killed with great speed. In a short time, the windswept mountain fortress of Masada was home to only ten remaining Zealots of the former 1,000 Jewish holdouts. Gathering together once again, their grizzly work nearly completed, the ten warriors drew lots a second time, this time to determine which among them would kill the remaining nine, then, take his own life.

After the lots were selected, one man was given the final duty of ending the Jewish resistance at Masada. He took his sword and sliced the throats of his nine fellow

Knowing that they could not escape defeat at the hands of the Romans, the Jews at Masada chose to commit mass suicide rather than be captured. First, the men killed their wives and children, and then a group of ten men were selected to kill all the other men. In the end, one man slit the throats of the nine remaining and then killed himself.

warriors. Then, left alone, perhaps remembering how Josephus had spared his own life following the Jotapata siege, this man of honor took his sword and "drove [it] clean through his own body and fell dead beside his family."

The next morning, when the Romans began their march up the long ramp to the broken wall of Masada, they expected a long, bloody day of desperate fighting. As they crossed the gangways from the ramp into the Jewish compound, however, they met the eerie silence of death rather than fierce warriors. There would be no fight after all. From the smoking rubble, seven survivors—two women and five children—emerged from the entrance of one of the large water reservoirs and revealed themselves to the Romans. In time they would tell the story of Eleazar Ben Ya'ir, and of the resolve of the Masada defenders to refuse to accept slavery for their families. To the Romans who found them, the Zealots represented "nobility and [an] utter contempt for death." After seven months of a grueling siege, the Romans had finally taken Masada. The Jewish rebellion was over. Years of bloody conquest were at an end. The Romans would take no prisoners from the hilltop fortress that day. They would leave the mountaintop empty-handed. The Jews had snatched the final act of victory from the conquering Roman army.

Masada, Archaeology, and Josephus

Professor Yadin's archaeological efforts revealed much about the history of the mountain site at Masada. At the heart of the excavation, though, was the drive to find out whether the story of the siege and the deaths of the Jewish Zealots in the first century A.D. had occurred in the way Josephus had described. The archaeologists were delighted to be able to confirm many of the details of the Josephus story.

While excavating Herod's bathhouse, workers uncovered the skeletal remains of three people who had huddled together in death, including a man, a woman, and a child, just as Josephus had described the suicide of the Zealot families. Workers found Jewish coins dating to A.D. 67 and 68, matching the early years of the Jewish revolt. Ashes were everywhere in the ruined buildings, a sign of sweeping fires. Weapons dating from the Jewish revolt period were also excavated, including bronze arrows and the remains of shields, as well as armor. In storerooms, the diggers found many clay jars of food, just as Josephus had said. At the site where the Snake Path emerged at the mountaintop, workers unearthed a pile of large stones, weighing 100 pounds (45 kilograms) each. Such stones had been hurled down on the Romans during the siege. Other evidence of Jewish occupation during the first century were also uncovered. Beneath the floor of the Masada synagogue, Yadin found the remains of a Torah scroll, the most sacred writings of the Jews.

Yet not every discovery made at Masada matches completely with Josephus' account. For one, only about 25 skeletons were unearthed by archaeologists. If nearly 1,000 people took part in the mass suicide, as Josephus claimed, where are their bodies? Some historians believe that many of the defenders at Masada had already left the mountain before or during the siege.

Another important discovery made at Masada, however, does seem to indicate the accuracy of Josephus's tale of Jewish heroics and the final suicide pact. This find was made one day when a worker dug up 11 *ostraca*, broken pieces (shards) of pottery with Hebrew writing on them. When the pieces were examined closely, the writing revealed the names, or more often, nicknames, of 11 different people. The shards include such names as "Fatso," "the baker's son," and "the guy from the valley." One of the names was that of the Zealots' leader, Ben Ya'ir. The archaeologists may have located the lots the men had cast to determine which Zealot warriors would execute their brothers in arms at the end of the siege.

than Yadin, though. He was a military man by experience who had served in the Israeli army during the Israeli War of Independence in 1948. Yadin had even climbed the Masada site as a boy.

Because Masada was just as remote in the twentieth century as it had been in the first century, Yadin had to figure out details such as how to get water and electricity to the site. Yadin flew in a helicopter over Masada to help him observe the site and make his plans. He also got help from the Israeli army. Israeli soldiers helped build a road to the site as well as construct staircases that led to the summit. Generators supplied electricity. Water was delivered to Masada through an abandoned oil pipeline.

Once everything was in place to support a team of diggers, Yadin set his workers to the task of excavating the ruins at Masada. The archaeological work at the mountain lasted from 1963 through 1964. Before the work was completed, 20,000 workers, most of them volunteers, had contributed their labor. At any given time, at least 300 people were on-site.

The ruins of Masada revealed many secrets. Herod's three-tier Hanging Palace was unearthed and examined. On the floors of the terraces, the archaeologists found mosaic patterns that had been common in Rome during the Herodian period. They also discovered the remains of columns and wall paintings in Roman designs. Fragments of wine bottles were inscribed with the words: *To King Herod of Judea*. The workers also unearthed the remains of the fifth-century chapel that had been built by Byzantine monks.

Yadin's excavations found much evidence that confirmed a good deal of Josephus's story. Through these archaeological discoveries and the words of Josephus, the story of Jewish courage in the face of overwhelming opposition from the strongest empire on Earth and the legend of how they fought to the death for their homeland during the sieges at Jotapata, Jerusalem, and Masada, lives on 2,000 years later.

1900 B.C.   Patriarch Abraham migrates from his home in Ur and settles in Canaan.

1400s B.C.   The early Hebrew people are led out of Egyptian slavery by Moses and take up residence in the land of Canaan.

1020s–920s B.C.   The period of the united Kingdom of Israel witnesses the rule of Kings Saul, David, and Solomon; Solomon erects the first Holy Temple in Jerusalem.

922 B.C.   The kingdom of Israel divides, each led by its own king; the ten northern tribes maintain the kingdom of Israel, while the tribes of Benjamin and Judah create a southern kingdom called Judah.

700s B.C.   The people of the northern kingdom of Israel are overrun by an aggressive people to the north, the Assyrians; many are taken into captivity and scattered throughout the ancient Near East.

1400 B.C.
The early Hebrew people are led out of Egyptian slavery by Moses and take up residence again in the land of Canaan.

1020–920s B.C.
Period of the rule of Israelite kings Saul, David, and Solomon.

1900 B.C.
Hebrew patriarch Abraham migrates from his home in Ur of Mesopotamia and settles in Canaan.

700s B.C.
Northern kingdom of Israel is overrun by the Assyrians.

2000 B.C.   **800 B.C.**

922 B.C.
Kingdom of Israel divides into northern kingdom of Israel and southern kingdom of Judah.

Timeline

580s B.C. The southern kingdom of Judah falls to the Babylonians; Mesopotamian invaders destroy the sacred temple in Jerusalem.

539 B.C. Persian King Cyrus defeats the Babylonians and inherits the dispossessed people known as the Jews; Cyrus allows the Jews to return to their homeland and rebuild their temple in Jerusalem.

520–445 B.C. The Jews return to Judah and rebuild their temple and the walls of the city of Jerusalem.

330s B.C. Macedonian ruler Alexander the Great marches east and captures Judea and Jerusalem; many Jews become Hellenized, taking on many aspects of Greek culture, thinking, and philosophy.

320 B.C. Egyptian ruler Ptolemy I captures Jerusalem and begins a reign over the Jews that will last for a century.

580s B.C.
The southern kingdom falls to the Babylonians. Temple in Jerusalem is destroyed.

540 B.C.
Persian King Cyrus defeats Babylonians and inherits the Jews, whom he allows to return to Jerusalem.

134–63 B.C.
Palestine ruled by the Hasmonaean Dynasty.

160s B.C.
The Maccabean Revolt destroys the power of the Seleucids and Syrians over Palestine.

A.D. 37
Birth of Jewish historian Josephus.

A.D. 41–44
Grandson of Herod the Great, Herod Agrippa I, rules Jews on behalf of Roman Empire.

500 B.C.   A.D. 100

330s B.C.
Alexander the Great captures Judea and Jerusalem.

198 B.C.
The Seleucids defeat the Ptolemies and take control of Palestine from the Seleucids.

63 B.C.
Hasmonaean Dynasty falls as the Roman General Pompey occupies the city of Jerusalem.

37–4 B.C.
Era of the reign of Herod the Great, King of the Jews, Great building projects erected during this period.

A.D. 72–73
Siege and fall of Masada.

A.D. 70
Jewish Revolt leads to the destruction of Jerusalem.

198 B.C.	The Seleucids defeat the Ptolemies and gain control of Palestine; the Hellenization of the Jews continues.
160s B.C.	Maccabean Revolt destroys the power of the Seleucids and the Syrians over Palestine.
134–63 B.C.	Palestine is under the direction of the Hasmonaean Dynasty; this era of Jewish history witnesses the administrations of five rulers, beginning with the son of Simon Maccabeus, John Hyrcanus I.
63 B.C.	The Hasmonaean Dynasty falls as the Roman General Pompey occupies the city of Jerusalem; Palestine remains under Roman domination for the next 200 years.
37–4 B.C.	Era of the reign of Herod the Great, king of the Jews; during his reign, Herod builds the palaces, baths, walls, and fortifications on the desert summit at Masada.
10 B.C.	Herod dedicates his new Holy Temple in Jerusalem, although the religious site is not completed until A.D. 63.
A.D. 37	Birth of the Jewish historian Josephus.
A.D. 41–44	Grandson of Herod the Great, Herod Agrippa I, rules as the king of the Jews with the sanction of the Roman Empire.
A.D. 48	Spontaneous Jewish uprising in the city of Jerusalem against the authority of the Roman Empire; the rebellion is crushed and many Jewish rebels are crucified.
A.D. 66	Another Jewish revolt breaks out, leading to the Roman destruction of the city of Jerusalem, including the Holy Temple.
Summer A.D. 67	The siege of Jotapata takes place, resulting in the destruction of the city by the Romans.
A.D. 70	Destruction of the Jewish Temple in Jerusalem, as well as of the city itself, at the hands of the Romans.
A.D. 72–73	The siege of Masada takes place, resulting in the murders and suicides of the entire Zealot garrison encamped on the summit.

CHAPTER 1, THE PEOPLE OF YAHWEH

Page 15:   "The atmosphere surrounding . . ."
             H. H. Ben-Sasson, ed. *A History of the
             Jewish People*. Cambridge, MA:
             Harvard University Press, 1976, p. 203.

Page 16:   "the offering of the traditional . . ."
             Martin Noth, *The History of Israel*.
             New York: Harper & Row, Publishers,
             1958, p. 366.

CHAPTER 2, HEROD BUILDS MASADA

Page 29:   "For the report goes . . ." Geraldine
             Rosenfield, *The Heroes of Masada*. The
             Melton Research Center of the Jewish
             Theological Seminary of America. A
             Publicationof the United Synagogue
             Commission on Jewish Education,
             1968, p. 13.

Page 31:   "There was a rock . . ." Ibid.

CHAPTER 3, THE JEWS RISE UP

Page 38:   "He went out . . ." Peter Connolly, *A
             History of the Jewish People in the time of
             Jesus*. New York: Peter Bedrick Books,
             1983, p. 60.

Page 41:   "plundered the land . . ." Martin Noth,
             The History of Israel. New York: Harper
             & Row, Publishers, 1958, p. 435.

Page 41:   "boasted openly . . ." Alfred H. Tamarin,
             *Revolt in Judea: The Road to Masada:
             The eyewitness account by Flavius
             Josephus of the Roman campaign against
             Judea, the destruction of the Second
             Temple, and the heroism of Masada*. New
             York: Four Winds Press, 1968, p. 43.

Page 42:   "The following day . . ." Connolly,
             p. 70.

Page 43:   "The rebels were now . . ." Noth, p. 436.

Page 44:   "They put the king's . . ." Tamarin,
             p. 48.

Page 46:   "the people massacred . . ." Ibid.,
             pp. 49, 51.

Page 46:   "Swarming through the hills . . ."
             Connolly, p. 72.

CHAPTER 4, THE SIEGE AT JOTAPATA

Page 53:   "green wicker and layers . . ." Peter
             Connolly, *A History of the Jewish People
             in the time of Jesus*. New York: Peter
             Bedrick Books, 1983, p. 79.

Page 54:   "I summoned all the . . ." Alfred H.
             Tamarin, *Revolt in Judea: The Road
             to Masada: The eyewitness account by
             Flavius Josephus of the Roman campaign
             against Judea, the destruction of the
             Second Temple, and the heroism of
             Masada*. New York: Four Winds
             Press, 1968, p. 66.

Page 54:   "To deceive the Romans . . ." Ibid.

Page 57:   "The wall gave way . . ." Yigael Yadin
             and Gerald Gottlieb, *The Story of
             Masada*. New York: Random House,
             1969, p. 114.

Page 57:   "Hand-to-hand fighting . . ." Tamarin,
             p. 66.

Page 58:   "When day broke . . ." Yadin and
             Gottlieb, p. 117.

Page 59:   "ventured forth . . ." Tamarin,
             p. 68.

Page 59:   "threatened me if I made . . ." Ibid.,
             p. 69.

CHAPTER 5, DESTRUCTION IN JERUSALEM

Page 65:   "I maintain that it was . . ." Alfred H.
             Tamarin, *Revolt in Judea: The Road
             to Masada: The eyewitness account by
             Flavius Josephus of the Roman campaign
             against Judea, the destruction of the
             Second Temple, and the heroism of
             Masada*. New York: Four Winds
             Press, 1968, p. 104.

Page 66:   "Titus . . .ordered his main army . . ."
             Ibid., p. 99.

Page 67–68: "Titus delegated me . . ." Ibid., p. 110.

Page 68:   "When one of these. . ." Peter Connolly,
             *A History of the Jewish People in the time
             of Jesus*. New York: Peter Bedrick
             Books, 1983, p. 86.

Page 71:   "so completely leveled . . ." Ibid.,
             pp. 127–128.

Page 72–73: "Masses of prisoners . . ." Ibid., p. 90.

Page 73:   "No pity was shown . . ." Tamarin,
             p. 122.

Page 74:   "Jerusalem was reduced . . ." Neil
             Waldman, *Masada*. New York: Morrow
             Junior Books, 1998, p. 19.

Page 74:   "great golden table . . ." Ibid., p. 20.

Page 74:   "A group of Roman . . ." Ibid., p. 21.

Page 75:   "immense height and . . ." Tamarin,
             p. 137.

CHAPTER 6, THE LAST STRONGHOLD

Page 78: "Now that the entire . . ." Yigael Yadin and Gerald Gottlieb, *The Story of Masada*. New York: Random House, 1969, p. 117.

Page 78–79: "The interior of the palace . . ." Alfred H. Tamarin, *Revolt in Judea: The Road to Masada: The eyewitness account by Flavius Josephus of the Roman campaign against Judea, the destruction of the Second Temple, and the heroism of Masada*. New York: Four Winds Press, 1968, pp. 141, 143.

Page 79: "arms of every description . . ." Ibid., p. 143.

Page 80: "encamped at a spot . . ." Ibid., p. 140.

Page 82: "[Silva] ordered his troops . . ." Ibid., p. 144.

Page 83: "With huge pulleys . . ." Neil Waldman, *Masada*. New York: Morrow Junior Books, 1998, p. 29.

Page 83: "With difficulty, [Silva] succeeded . . ." Tamarin, p. 145.

Page 84: "destroy this inner wall . . ." Ibid.

Page 85: "Long ago, my brave . . ." Ibid., p. 146.

Page 85: "Did we, in truth . . ." Ibid.

Page 85: "But let us not pay . . ." Ibid., p. 147.

Page 86: "But the multitudes. . ." Ibid., p. 148.

Page 87: "They took their wives . . ." Ibid., p. 150.

Page 87: "they offered their own . . ." Ibid., p. 151.

Page 89: "drove [it] clean through . . ." Ibid.

Page 89: "nobility and [an] utter . . ." Ibid.

Ben-Sasson, H. H., ed. *A History of the Jewish People*. Cambridge, MA: Harvard University Press, 1976.

Ben-Yehuda, Nachman. *The Masada Myth: Collective Memory and Mythmaking in Israel*. Madison: University of Wisconsin Press, 1995.

Cornfield, Gaalyah. *This Is Masada*. New York: Scribner, 1967.

Cross, Robin, ed. *Warfare, A Chronological History*. Secaucus, NJ: Wellfleet Press, 1991.

Durant, Will. *Caesar and Christ: A History of Roman civilization and of Christianity from their beginnings to A.D. 325*. New York: Simon and Schuster, 1944.

Grant, M. *The Jews in the Roman World*. London: Weidenfeld & Nicolson, 1973.

Hall, John F., and John W. Welch, eds. *Masada and the World of the New Testament*. Provo, UT: BYU Studies, Brigham Young University, 1997.

Johnson, Paul. *A History of the Jews*. New York: Harper & Row, Publishers, 1987.

Kokkinos, Nikos. *The Herodian Dynasty: Origins, Role in Society and Eclipse*. Journal for the Study of the Pseudepigrapha. Supplement Series 30. Sheffield, England: Sheffield Academic Press, 1998.

The New Oxford Annotated Bible, containing the Old and New Testaments. New York: Oxford University Press, 1991.

Noth, Martin. *The History of Israel*. New York: Harper & Row, Publishers, 1958.

Richardson, Peter. *Herod: King of the Jews and Friend of the Romans*. Minneapolis: Fortress Press, 1999.

Rosenfield, Geraldine. *The Heroes of Masada*. The Melton Research Center of the Jewish Theological Seminary of America. A Publication of the United Synagogue Commission on Jewish Education, 1968.

Sachar, Abram Leon. *A History of the Jews*. New York: Knopf, 1968.

Smallwood, Mary. *The Jews under Roman Rule*. Kinderhoook, NY: E. J. Brill, 1976.

Tamarin, Alfred H. *Revolt in Judea: The Road to Masada: The eyewitness account by Flavius Josephus of the Roman campaign against Judea, the destruction of the Second Temple, and the heroism of Masada*. New York: Four Winds Press, 1968.

Yadin, Yigael. Masada: *Herod's Fortress and the Zealots' Last Stand*. New York: Random House, 1966.

Connolly, Peter. *A History of the Jewish People in the Time of Jesus.* New York: Peter Bedrick Books, 1983.

Miklowitz, Gloria D. *Masada: The Last Fortress.* Grand Rapids, MI: Eerdmans Books for Young Readers, 1998.

Yadin, Yigael, and Gerald Gottlieb. *The Story of Masada.* (Retold for young readers) New York: Random House, 1969.

Waldman, Neil. *Masada.* New York: Morrow Junior Books, 1998.

VIDEO

Mysteries of the Bible III, *The Greatest Stories: Masada*. Multimedia Entertainment and Hearst/ABC/NBC Arts and Entertainment Networks, 1994.

page:

2: Reprinted from "Masada and the World of the New Testament," John Hall and John Welsh, eds., BYU Studies, Brigham Young University, Provo, Utah
7: Nathan Benn/Corbis
18: Michael Kevin Daly/Corbis
22: Erich Lessing/Art Resource, NY
30: Alinari/Art Resource, NY
33: Richard T. Nowitz/Corbis
36: National Gallery Collection; By kind permission of the Trustees of the National Gallery, London/Corbis
45: Richard T. Nowitz/Corbis

48: SEF/Art Resource, NY
50: Erich Lessing/Art Resource, NY
56: New York Public Library/Art Resource, NY
60: Giraudon/Art Resource, NY
62: Historical Picture Archive/Corbis
69: Alinari/SEAT/Art Resource, NY
72: Cameraphoto/Art Resource, NY
76: Richard T. Nowitz/Corbis
81: Bubbu Mays/Corbis
88: Bettmann/Corbis
90: Ted Spiegel/Corbis
92: Farrell Graham/Corbis

Cover: Nathan Benn/Corbis

TIM MCNEESE is an Associate Professor of History at York College in Nebraska. He is the author of more than fifty books on everything from Egyptian Pyramids to American Indians. Processor McNeese graduated from York College with his Associate in Arts degree, as well as Harding University where he received his Bachelor of Arts degree in history and political science. He received his Master of Arts degree in history from Southwest Missouri State University. He has been a teacher of middle and high school students, as well as college students, for the past 27 years. His reading audiences range from elementary through adult. Professor McNeese's writing career has earned him a citation on the "Something About the Author" reference work. He is married to Beverly McNeese who teaches English at York College.